Boo!

Tony Kearney

authorHOUSE®

Best wishes,
Tony Kearney

AuthorHouse™ UK Ltd.
500 Avebury Boulevard
Central Milton Keynes, MK9 2BE
www.authorhouse.co.uk
Phone: 08001974150

First published by AuthorHouse 2/18/2010

ISBN: 978-1-4490-4982-9 (sc)

This book is printed on acid-free paper.

This book is dedicated to the next person you meet, whose life you can make better by either what you do or what you don't do.

Contents

Introduction   xi

Are You Alive or Merely Existing?   1

Are You Fit For Purpose?   7

Don't be an Asshole All Your Life!   11

Opinion   17

Researching the Meaning of Life   19

The Illusion of Choice   27

The Illusion of Difference   31

It's All About Me!   35

Stop Trying to Make a Difference   45

Can one person make a difference?   53

How to Make a Difference   57

Self-Sabotage   77

How to be a Subversive   83

What Do You Want?   87

The Feng Shui of You   93

You become what you think about.or
You don't become what you don't think about.   101

Self-Leadership   113

Natural Confidence   121

Know Thyself   129

What Do You Represent?   135

What Drives You?	143
Spontaneity Training	147
Will	153
You Only See What You Have Trained Your Eyes to See	159
It's Simply a Case of Mind Over Matter	165
It's Time to think about your Epitaph!	169
Shock	171
Life's Little Imperfections	181
Why Not Learn to Play the Synthesiser?	185
Attachment and Detachment	191
It's Time for a Brainwave	195
Don't listen to all the Hype, Propaganda andBullshit – Especially from Oneself!	203
Drugs Can Seriously Damage Your Health– TV and Newspapers that is.	211
The Matter with or the Matter of Relationships	225
Language	233
The Most Important Word Ever	241
Indifference	245
Intelligence	249
Assimilation	261
Interpretation	267
Talent/Latent	273
Genius	279
Attitude	283

Inspiration 289

Illumination 293

Passion and Compassion 297

Being a Healer 305

Immunity 317

How to Be your Own Saviour 327

Seven Pillars of Belief 331

Inhibit the Habit and Don't Inhabit
the Inhibition 341

Innocence and Guilt 347

The Truth 353

Conception 355

Can You Do it? 361

You Attract What You Act 363

Being Settled 371

Watch Out for Entropy – It Could Kill You! 377

Epilogue 379

About the Author 381

Introduction

Whilst on a trip to America a few years ago to do some public talks about my last book – *Who Owns the Future?* - a friend recommended a book to me called *The Tipping Point* by Malcolm Gladwell. *

This was interesting to me because I had been talking in the lectures of the fact that real and fundamental change cannot, and does not, happen until matters reach a moment of poised criticality. This is where all that has happened before suddenly cascades into a new elevation or polarity. It's a bit like the built up pressure that causes a dam to break.

Having heard my talk in New York City, my friend recommended that I get hold of a copy of The Tipping Point. So, off I went to Barnes and Noble (my favourite book store, thanks to the very civilised way one can browse and read in comfort and leisure) to find a copy.

When I got there I decided to browse first rather than simply ask at the Information Desk for a copy. I then went through the various sections where I thought it might be found without success, all the time browsing in case I found another book that I might want to read. In this, if you pardon the pun, I was clearly the author of my own misfortune for not being sufficiently focused in my search, and what that then caused. Be warned, such lack of focus could cause similar things to happen to you!

Eventually I ended up in the self-help / personal development section, and this seemed to be the biggest section of the whole store. There seemed to be books on any and every aspect of self improvement imaginable, from Feng Shui for Animals to Tantric Sex Yoga, from Astrological Chakra Balancing to Cosmic Ordering for Vegans, to Finding Your Inner Alien and everything and anything in between!

As I browsed through this kaleidoscopic potpourri of promised enlightenment, a creeping sense of claustrophobia began to manifest in me. My breathing became shallower, my confusion levels increased, and my sense of how to navigate my way out of the self help section of the bookstore became worryingly wayward!

How ironic that this could be caused by a sea of self help books, I thought.

When finally, via the help of the maps section, I managed to escape this plethora of mind numbing mentoring and life coaching self improvement, I made my way gingerly to the Help desk and asked the clerk to help me find the book I had come to buy.

The clerk was able to do this very quickly indeed. So I bought the book and carefully made my way out of the store for a chance to regroup and gather myself to myself. I headed for Central Park for a walk to recover and also to quietly sit on a park bench and read my new book. This I did, and then afterwards went about the rest of my day. (*By the way, for those interested in the phenomena of trends and pivotal change I thoroughly recommend The

Tipping Point as a most excellently researched and well written treatise on the subject.)

Afterwards I reflected on my experience in the bookstore and wondered whether it was unique to me. After all, the self help / self improvement genre is one of the biggest and, of course, most profitable niche markets within the book industry.

Perhaps this is simply because there is so much wrong with how people live their lives that they therefore need continual help in order to get some kind of grip on who they are and how to get to where they want to go?

However, I did not sense that this was the case, but rather that there was something deeper at play that needed researching.

For the feeling I had was one of increasing confusion rather than greater clarity. With so many options available on sale, where was a person to start in treating the many maladies from which they were clearly suffering?

At this point a realisation began to dawn on me, and this was that more and more information could, in fact, be harmful rather than helpful; because it was more and more about less and less. In fact most of it was very *me* based and failed to give context and location to the placement of a life within any kind of bigger picture. Nor did it give any sense of integrated location that all is connected to all, and that all affects all.

With this in mind I then decided to try and write something myself in an attempt, if nothing else, to relocate myself inside some kind of reality check. Also, I felt that it would help me cope better the next time I felt strong enough to visit the self help section of Barnes & Noble in that hopefully I wouldn't have a panic attack or turn into some kind of mumbling, bumbling, psychobabble spouting freak.

For my sense was that many of the books on sale actually add to, rather than lessen, the confusion facing people today when trying to find meaning and value inside their busy and hectic lives.

So this book represents an attempt to highlight some important considerations for people living such busy lives, offering some thoughts and ideas, plus practical tips, to help find some crucial alignments for life.

But, before embarking on that journey:

Within this search for location, perhaps the first place to start from is simply that; in other words, where is a person actually beginning their journey from? What is the truth of their situation as they embark on any journey of self discovery and self realisation?

As I walked through the streets of New York City that day, I felt that most people were actually awake / asleep as opposed to asleep / asleep. They may have been going about their obviously busy and frenetic lives at quite a pace, (New York sure does buzz at that level) yet somehow what looked out of their eyes was something mostly robotic and not really awake to the inner life truth of what their life could actually be like. (This feeling doesn't say something specific about New York alone, it should be said, for I experienced the exact same sense when I flew to London a few days later.)

Perhaps somewhere within life's demands and relentless noise there is an oasis within which a person can, if nothing else, find themselves. This book represents an attempt to help find the 'X spot'.

And if you are in Barnes and Noble flicking through this book in trying to decide whether or not you should buy it, and you suddenly begin to feel slightly panicky and paranoid and don't know where or who you are, then my advice is to put it back on the shelf and get out while you can. This book clearly isn't for you!

But if you are looking for a series of starters, prompters, ideas, a shock or two along the way perhaps, then *Boo!* might just have something for you. The idea of the title is that we all need a wake up call every now and then in order to stay awake to the possibility and challenge that living presents to each and every one of us.

So ... *Boo!* not in the sense of voicing one's disapproval, but in the sense of Carpe Deum (seize the day). If the opportunity that the latter presents is loved and lived then any need for the former evaporates into the ether from where it came in the first place.

If we wake up to the possibility of what our lives truly present to us then fulfilment becomes a real, tangible and thrilling possibility.

As Soren Kierkergard said, "Life can only be understood backwards, but it must be lived forwards."

Are You Alive or Merely Existing?

*It is not death that a man should fear, but
he should fear never beginning to live.*

Marcus Aurelius

*If you shoot for the stars and hit the moon,
it's alright. But you've got to shoot for
something. A lot of people don't even shoot.*

Confucius

There is a famous story in the Bible (Luke: Chapter 9) where Jesus is talking to his disciples. He tells them that they need to come away with him in order to receive some important instruction that day.

One of the disciples says that he can't come because he has to help bury a dead relative.

Jesus's reaction to this is to say to the disciple, 'Let the dead bury the dead.'

The clear meaning within this comment is that in Jesus's view there were people in the world who, although physically fit and healthy, were spiritually dead and therefore of little or no consequence.

1

In modern terms they would be classed as robots or automatons.

In his view it was far more important for the disciples to be with him because he was alive and carrying the very essence of what it meant to be truly living. The disciples, therefore, would be well served by spending as much time with him as possible in order to catch as much of his knowledge and wisdom as they could.

Another word for this kind of empty vacancy, albeit a rather extreme one, is the term 'zombie'. Many a film has been made about the invasion of the zombies, or something similar, and if well made they really do have the power to shock and frighten.

However, the question needs to be asked as to whether a person has aspects of this robotic, automaton or zombie like behaviour going on in them for some, if not a lot, of the time?

This is often evidenced by a person having a very habitual and fixed pattern in their life with things being mostly the same all the time and rather predictable. They are often bored, see many of the things that they have to do in their life as a boring drudgery, and they have very little spontaneity or sparkle.

The alarm goes off to start another day, and often their first thought is that they are tired and don't want to go to work - but they have to. So they drift off to the shower, have a quick snack for breakfast, and sometime after that they tend to actually wake up because most of the activities they have been doing up until then have been done on autopilot.

In fact, almost everything they do is on autopilot.

This indeed is a malaise of modern living, for with the speed of everything it is hard for a person to even think about what it is they are actually doing. Mostly we are forever trying to find new ways of doing things quicker so that we can get some more time to do something else even quicker!

For example, the cooking and preparation of food today, is as often as not, done by someone other than the family members. With the rise of takeaway food and so-called TV dinners, very little time is spent in preparing food for the family meal, and so there is little, if any, appreciation of what goes into its preparation.

This is further compounded by the fact that often the evening meal is eaten whilst watching TV rather than over the dinner table with conversation and exchange about the day and other matters of family importance. Thus the food for the body and the food for the brain combine to make a very unhealthy diet, both physically and mentally.

Often the TV is simply switched on as a matter of habit, and with the advent of satellite TV, there are now countless channels of brain-numbing dross to watch rather than the previous mere handful. The only discussion that seems to take place is over who should have right to possession of the remote control and what drivel they should get to choose that everyone else should watch.

Quite often this results in channel surfing, which further compounds the problem because no one gets to watch much of anything. In the desperate search to find something to watch nothing is found so the search must go on. The alternative - which is to turn the beast off and have a conversation - never enters anyone's head, for what is there to talk about?

It is therefore little wonder that people's attention spans get shorter and shorter. This is because their lifestyles do not in any way encourage its development and, in fact, continually undermine it.

Figures show that the number of children with Attention Deficit Hyperactivity Disorder (ADHD) increases every year. This often relates to lifestyle issues, from diet to family pressures, and is regarded by some as being as important an influence as genetic inheritance. In fact, often the reason a child has ADHD is that their parents or parent has ADHD in some shape or form and they themselves are unable to give the child the right kind of quality of attention.

Of course the stretch in this is quite difficult at times because many families need two incomes in order to support their lifestyle. So when children come along decisions need to be made about how to go forward. This inevitably leads to the need for compromises.

Because of this the amount of quality time that a family spends together becomes less and less because everyone is being pulled in different directions. This in turn leads to problems and difficulties. But having made certain decisions as to how the various family members' roles will be divided, it is then difficult to change the balances because this can be seen as either a sign of failure or of someone having to compromise more than someone else.

This applies not only to families, but also to individuals who may seemingly appear to be independent. The same issues inevitably apply, just in a different form.

For example, an individual not in a 'relationship' has a whole different set of pressures and stresses to face; from how to get a partner, which places and parties they can go to on their own, to family pressures to settle down, and so much more.

The point of all this is to emphasise the fact that it is so easy for a person to be consumed by the life of merely going on, of existing; drifting through life with attendant highs and lows, but mostly within the band of expendable experience.

This is not living.

To which the question naturally comes: Well what is living then?

To which the answer can only be: To try and find out what real living is actually like.

You may say that this is hardly helpful, but every endeavour begins with a try that is beyond the usual habitual patterns of the mundane, ordinary and conformist patterns of simply existing.

Read on and you just might find something that rings true for you.

Are You Fit For Purpose?

*We have two ears and one tongue so that
we would listen more and talk less.*

Diogenes

*The flighty purpose never is o'ertook
unless the deed go with it.*

Shakespeare

This chapter begins with a question: Do you think that there is anything contractual in living a life, i.e. are there any inherent obligations that go with the fact of simply being a human being? If so, what do you think those obligations and duties might be?

If life is a contract between a person and other things, then it would be useful to know how to think about:

a. what those obligations might be and
b. what it might take to perform them
c. what exactly are those 'other things'

One could start with considering the nature of the law and how it thinks about performance of contractual obligations. But before we start be warned, it could get complicated! But there are some useful and interesting principles to consider here that do apply to the business of living.

So, in law there are three basic levels for the performance of a contract between the contracting parties. These three levels are:

1. To use all **reasonable** skill and care in the performance of the services. The standard required here by law is: what would a reasonable man (or woman) expect each party to do in order to meet their obligations under the contract? What would be fair, reasonable and proportionate in the circumstances?

2. That the party will use their **best endeavours** in performing their obligations under the contract. If this standard is accepted, it then requires the party agreeing to it to do their very best every time, regardless of any extenuating circumstances.

3. That something will be **fit for purpose**. This simply means that something is either fit for purpose or it isn't. This is known as a strict and absolute obligation, and there are no excuses and no let-out clauses.

So that's the area of law and the standards required in the performance of a legal contract, but how might this apply to the area of personal development?

Well, countless millions of years of organic life on Earth have led to the development of the human form and all its attributes and capabilities that we now see. By a process of natural selection (or intelligent design, if Darwin's Theory sticks in your craw) we now find ourselves with a human design and model that is clearly fit for purpose. It is pretty hard to think of a way that one would change the human design in order to make it better for us to live our lives here. (Although ask a group of 7 year olds how they would improve the design they sometimes come up with some great ideas!)

Nature and/or Creation are very clever at designing life forms that work, and they build into those forms the ability to change and adapt to their environment() as required.

With this in mind, the question arises: For what purpose is the human 'designed'? (And if you are a Darwinian, the term 'designed' was put in quotation marks to illustrate that it is a concept rather than an article of faith.) Phew! You have to be so careful when talking about these matters.

Anyway, the question remains: What is the purpose of the human design?

Is there a purpose at all?

Are there levels to that purpose; for example physical, moral and spiritual?

And if there is a purpose, or purposes, to the human design, how would one go about using one's reasonable and best endeavours in using the design that one has been given to serve that purpose?

Assuming, therefore, that the human design is a blueprint for the purpose of what a human being is meant to be, do you use all reasonable endeavours in carrying out the contract of life as you perceive it to be? Are you as fair with your design as your design is fair with you?

Is there a contract between the design and the designer/what allowed the design to evolve?

If so, what is it and what level of performance criteria would you/do you agree to be bound by?

Fit for purpose?

Best endeavours?

Reasonable endeavours?

It's your choice, because the very fact of choice seems to be something that is inherent within the design itself.

Eating and drinking rubbish doesn't make the design work any better, and in fact undermines its ability to work at optimum.

Thinking rubbish doesn't help either.

Neither does behaving in a negative or selfish way.

What does seem to work is to use the design in the way that it was designed to be used and to make sure that it has a regular service.

This raises an interesting question, which is: what kind of service does the human design need to have to keep it in tip-top working order, and what kind of service does it need to give in order for a person to be able to regard themselves as being truly fit for purpose?

What do you think?

Don't be an Asshole All Your Life!

Nothing is more intolerable than to have to
admit to yourself your own errors.

Ludwig van Beethoven

Do you wish to be great?
Then begin by being.
Do you desire to construct a vast and lofty fabric?
Think first about the foundations of humility.
The higher your structure is to be,
the deeper must be its foundation.

Saint Augustine

The object of life is not to be on the side
of the majority, but to escape finding
oneself in the ranks of the insane.

Marcus Aurelius

OK, so this chapter assumes that you have been to
every empowerment course going, that you have been
mentored until you can't be mentored anymore, that you
have been coached so much that you missed the coach
home! Yet despite it all, you are really much the same as

you were before you spent the equivalent of the GDP of a small country trying to sort yourself out once and for all.

You have had your house exorcised, had the ley lines on which your house lies cleansed, Feng Shuied the place until everything was shipped out of the house, until there was nothing left inside because everything was 'impure'. Yet, despite your newfound minimalist, new age, chakra balanced state of equilibrium people still look at you as though you are a weirdo.

What's wrong with them all? Don't they see that you are now the answer to all their prayers? Why don't the heathens see the saviourial vibes that come off you with every breath you take? Why don't they all clamber over each other to offer you the thousands of opportunities that your deeply connected and religious state now merits? Don't they see that you hold every key to every door they may ever need to open?

No they don't.

And the reason they don't is that they have instincts, and their instincts are telling them that deep down beneath all the veneer, despite all these superficial external changes, that you are still basically the same asshole you always were. And even worse still, you are now a smug asshole!

For clouds of incense and the chanting of power mantras don't change a thing per se. Indeed they often make things worse because they can delude the person into thinking that they have made some fundamental changes, whereas in actual fact all the changes are only cosmetic.

The self-help industry is a multi-billion dollar enterprise and the number of things it can cure far outweighs the number of people on the planet. In fact, one of the most serious of these new diseases is called 'New Age Hypochondria' i.e. there has to be something wrong with you all the time. You therefore need to constantly attend encounter groups where only re-birthing and squirmingly uncomfortable 'confessional' processes can help cleanse the patient of all the toxic build up accumulated both in this life and the many previous lives lived in Egypt as a Pharaoh and as an Native American shaman. (Why does no one ever remember their past life as a toilet cleaner?)

For once something is 'fixed' it can only highlight something else that is wrong. And so the cycle continues as the person furthers their journey on the never ending treadmill that goes round in ever decreasing circles until the person disappears up their own backside!

Which brings us to the title of this chapter.

If a person is full from having eaten too much, then they need to excrete before they take any more food in, and what they need to excrete is what they no longer need. In short, they need to have a crap to get rid of some crap.

The body is pretty efficient in this crap elimination process, although it struggles to cope sometimes, especially if there is nothing other than crap that comes into the system. It is coded to assimilate the necessary vitamins and minerals from the food that is ingested and to then eliminate the toxic by-products from the system. The kidneys, for example, do this function by cleansing the body with fluids flushing through the system and eliminating waste products through the urine.

However, if a person doesn't eat anything other than junk food, and drinks nothing but sugar laden soft drinks, then the body is going to be put under tremendous pressure. Not only is there far too much toxic substance for the body to cope with, in terms of processing out, but also there are not enough quality nutriments entering the system to enable it to function properly.

As such there is a double whammy effect: too much crap to process out and not enough energy to do this effectively.

This is asshole behaviour. Yet millions of people do it all the time because they don't see that there is anything wrong with it. Otherwise, why would they do it? Or worse still, some people continue even though they know that it is a stupid thing to do and that it has already undermined their basic health platform.

This is compounded asshole behaviour!

So why do people do it?

The main reasons are ignorance and lack of discipline. The first can generally be explained by lack of education, and the second is easy enough to see, in that people are, for one reason or another, not able to stop themselves from behaving in a certain way. This can be due to the fact that they are addicted to a certain form of behaviour, or because they are basically too lazy or lack the will-power to change a behavioural pattern.

The truth is that they are in some form of denial and, in particular, they are in denial of the consequences of what that continued behavioural pattern might cause. For all the warnings in the world on cigarette packets won't stop some people from smoking. Sometimes a triple heart by-pass won't stop them smoking either. This easy to see principle applies to a multitude of behaviours, from drug addiction to alcohol abuse or gambling, to anger management, to self harming, and many other forms of negative behaviour.

What this chapter proposes is that before considering spending another fortune on finding the next steps towards the state of Nirvana, how about the idea of getting rid of some ballast?

After all, there are two ways that a balloon can gain more height: it can either burn some more of its precious fuel, or it can throw out some ballast, such as sand. Before burning the precious fuel it is usually best to consider throwing out some baggage, because if all the fuel is used too early then there will be none left later when the person may really need it. The trip will also be shorter rather than longer.

The analogy with the human condition is clear enough to see, for if a person uses too much fuel on the wrong things, then the chances are they will lead a less rewarding life, and in all probability a shorter one.

This again is asshole behaviour.

So what then are some of the types of baggage that a person can throw out of their balloon?

Here's an exercise to hopefully help with this process.

Write down a list of 5 unfortunate behavioural patterns that you know you have. (and don't try and get away with saying you have only two!) It can be anything from proneness to anger, propensity to sulk if things don't go your way, or perhaps a tendency to bully other people, or indeed allowing yourself to be bullied. It might be delusions of grandeur where you think you are the

Messiah and yet no one else realises this fact or it might be comfort eating. The size of the pattern doesn't matter. What matters is that it is real and that it applies to you.

Having written them down, then spend 15 minutes contemplating each pattern in turn for 3 minutes each.

Then spend another 15 minutes writing down things that you can actually do in respect of each of these unfortunate traits in order to lessen or ameliorate their affects. And there will be things you can do, because if you learned how to be an asshole, you can definitely learn how to unlearn it!

The counsel here is to find small, starter disciplines that will help get you on the journey of lessening their grip, rather than going for the knockout blow, for this usually only results in failure and disappointment.

Then spend a month putting your plan into action.

If you follow through on the plan, the chances are you will be less of an asshole by the end of the process. This will be a source of great joy, both for yourself and for everyone else who knows you!

This makes it definitely worth doing.

Plus, think of the money you will save by not having to go on all those courses! You will be able to donate it to a small country that has a GDP and actually needs the money.

Self-diagnosis is a wonderful tool. Self-remedy is the best cure.

Being an asshole wastes time and money and does no one any favours.

So by all means have one and use it as necessary – but try and avoid becoming one!

Opinion

Nothing exists except atoms and empty space;
everything else is opinion.

Democritus

Only two things are infinite, the universe and
human stupidity,
and I'm not sure about the former.

Albert Einstein

There is a saying in the world that 'everyone is entitled to their opinion'. But are they?

Clearly at basic level people are entitled, or at least permitted, to have an opinion because everyone does have one. It has also been said that 'opinions are like assholes – everyone's got one!'

Nobody would want to describe themselves as being an asshole, and yet the more opinions they have about things the more they probably act like one!

So, before proceeding ask yourself just how many opinions you really need in order to go on? Surely it can't be *that* many, can it?

Researching the Meaning of Life

*And remember, no matter where
you go, there you are.*

Confucius

*If we knew what we were doing,
it wouldn't be called research would it?*

Albert Einstein

Research is a wonderful, natural process, and is something all humans know how to do, right from the moment when each and every one of them draws their first breath.

Research into the meaning of life begins right there – in that very first moment. Research is not something academic or bookish. It is something humans innately and inherently know how to do. It is that vital, that raw, that real. It is only later that people come to think of research as something done by clever people in laboratories or other places of supposed higher learning.

At birth we are all faced with the same key fundamental questions, which are: Who am I? What am I? Why am I here? How am I meant to go on? What do I need and how do I get it? When a child is born it cannot articulate these questions in strict language formation other than possibly via a howling cry. Yet, in a sense, that is much more primal and real because they are coming from a burning desire that is seared into their soul and spirit life at the moment of birth itself. If people are not careful they can easily lose this driving intensity that makes demand to all and everything to give meaning and method to their very existence.

The way the world often depotentises this urge is by providing plenty of meaning of the wrong kind to occupy the space meant for the search for causal meaning. The nature of this urge to learn and grow needs to evolve with the person throughout their life. The basic question remains at the cornerstone of it all, which is: is there a meaning to life beyond simply existing?

When humans are born life is full of total meaning and experience, for they have not yet acquired grids of reference for anything. Everything from hunger to excreting is a total experience. For example, babies can sleep almost anywhere if they are tired, despite all sorts of noise and interference. However, as people get older they can no longer seem to ignore or block out such interference and can only sleep if certain conditions are present.

From birth onwards people develop grids for how to deal and interact with the world and everything in it. They recognise their mother and the bond that forms between them very quickly develops. They know that mother is a good person to know because her breast is where the food comes from! Slowly over time, more and more grids come into place as the child learns more about who they are, what their position in the family and society is, and what is expected of them.

Often this developing of grids can become more and more dominant in the person's life. The search for meaning, therefore, gets dampened down or squeezed out to the point where a person can think that they are an accountant or a policeman or a housewife, rather than thinking that this is simply something they do.

This sense of alienation from self is extremely common, for the education system seeks in many ways to put people in boxes or grids of conformity, causing them to identify with the box that they have been put into. It is hardly any wonder, therefore, that often later in life people start to question the worth and value of the life they have lived, for often in retrospect a person fails to see much meaning or point to it all.

This is also very prevalent among young people who may still be near to that original burning desire for meaning. Yet, looking forward, they often fail to see anything on the assembly line of modern cultural life offered to them that offers hope or context for this search for meaning. This can then lead to a sense of alienation and despair, and frequently what is termed 'anti-social behaviour' or even suicide.

Within this feature there needs to be a balance struck between the search for meaning on the one hand, and grids of behaviour on the other. Grids of the right kind are crucial in any developing life for they can and should offer location and direction towards finding deeper and greater meaning. They should operate like co-ordinate points on a map and indicate to the person:

a. where they have come from
b. where they are now
c. where they need to go next

Without grids people are lost. Without meaning they have no purpose.

It is important to state that meaning is not an absolute property in itself. What is meant by this? Meaning is just the like the person themselves; it grows according to experience had, not primarily according to what one does, although that is clearly a factor within it.

Two people can do exactly the same act or series of actions; for one person it has no meaning, and for the other it can connect them to something high and religious. This also distinguishes between one person saying that they have a job for a living and another saying they have found their true vocation in life.

This depends on how people are introduced to things and the ecology in which they are allowed to find meaning within what they do. If people live in an ecology of warmth and love and are encouraged to search out the truth and question things, then that creates a huge space into which they can grow.

If, on the other hand, they are met with too much definition as to who they are and what they can become, then this automatically shrinks their possibility – or at least creates a greater resistance against which they have to lean in pursuit of the truth. However, resistance itself is not necessarily a bad thing, for it often forms part of the natural growth of a sturdier line of genetic possibility. Most of the great lives of history have triumphed over adversity rather than having had an easy time of it.

Another way people are deceived about the meaning of life is that they are encouraged to find ways to make things more comfortable and self-satisfying with less and less struggle. This isn't saying that a life of pure asceticism is what is needed, for that is simply denial for its own sake. After abandoning his life of wealth and privilege for one of total asceticism, the Buddha found that he was no nearer the truth than he was in his previous life of privilege and indulgence. His new life of rejection of all things material was also a chimera that hid the truth from him just as effectively as having all his worldly wishes catered for did. It was when he discovered what was called *the third way* that he became the Buddha, the Enlightened One. Both previous paths were lines of resistance that enabled him to not be claimed by either of them, but to use them as leverage into spiritual enlightenment by the principle of non attachment.

This aspect of resistance is something both entirely natural and yet greatly misunderstood. Each living thing has to face its own resistance and rise above it, if it is to survive and flourish. This is neatly illustrated by a recent discovery made at the Biosphere in America. The Biosphere was designed to research the viability of building an earth-like ecology in a self-contained circumstance so that, if it worked, it could be used to help colonise other planets. Although why people would want to do that – when it is quite clear that the human form is designed solely for living on this planet and that all our bodily systems, like bones, blood and nerves, wouldn't survive long-term living somewhere away from Earth – has never really been properly addressed. However, that is another story!

Anyway, back to the Biosphere. What was discovered was that at first all the plants in the Biosphere absolutely flourished in their clean, bug-free ecology with optimum conditions of food, water, light and warmth. However, after a period of time, all the plants and trees started to suddenly whither and die. This completely baffled the scientists as there was no apparent reason for this. Finally they discovered the reason, and it was due to the fact that there was no wind in the Biosphere!

Without wind there was no resistance for the plants to work against as they grew upwards. Initially they grew quickly, but without the natural resistance that the wind offered they were not able to fashion a robust and sturdy constitution in themselves. Therefore, as they got taller this weak constitution, brought about by having had it too easy for too long, meant that they simply fell over and died.

This is a stunning and very important location to consider in researching the meaning of life. Resistance can manifest in very many ways and is different for each person. That is why it is so important for a person to know themselves.

Knowing oneself is far more than simply being self-aware. It involves assessing one's situation and environment, what influences and causes things to be the way they are, how things work, what is needed, how to respond, and much, much more. As John Donne said: *"No man is an island, each is a part of the mainland."* For all are influenced by the same forces that flow through the vine of Creation, yet each person has a unique journey to travel as they try to find the meaning of life for themselves in themselves.

There needs to be a sense of the unknown within this journey, for there is much more that is unknown about the Universe and Creation than is known. Consider what a tiny percentage of it can be seen, even on a cloudless night with a carpet of stars in the sky. Yet on some of those special occasions there is much more that people can *feel* about the meaning of life than can be explained by all the theologians, philosophers and scientists in the world put together.

Yet many people have a fear of the unknown, and this fear is largely trained into people as they look for their securities in life via material and temporal things. These things do have their place and importance, but if they are over emphasised then other more important issues must thereby be relegated.

People do find meaning in their life according to the values they place on things and according to the decisions they make. Unfortunately, for many people in the world the meaning in their life is in trying to find enough food to eat or water to drink just to survive. For others there is the uncertainty of not knowing if their lives will be ended by the ever present blight of war and terrorism. Killing other human beings in the furtherance of dogma and fundamentalism never adds value or merit to the meaning of life.

It is appreciated and understood that sometimes these issues are complex and multi-faceted, but nevertheless the point is valid. For surely human beings have not only the possibility but also the right to enjoy much more than mere existence in their pursuit of the meaning of life?

Within this principle there is something to be understood about the notion of Karma in its more esoteric considerations. According to what a person builds in their life, they attract/repel certain forces and influences on their journey and also beyond.

What a person processes they get to keep.

What a person likes they become like.

What a person shares they grow.

If they connect to where high things come from then that's where they go.

The Illusion of Choice

Choose always the way that seems the best,
however rough it may be; custom will soon
render it easy and agreeable.

Pythagoras

God offers to every mind its choice
between truth and repose.

Ralph Waldo Emerson

One of the great illusions in the world today is that people think they have a real choice where the purpose and direction of their lives are concerned.

For after all, a person can go to the supermarket and choose which brand of soap or washing powder they wish to use. They can choose what they want to eat, what they want to wear, what they want to watch on television, what kind of car they want to drive, which school they send their children to, where they go on holiday, and so much more. Well, actually there are billions of people in the world who can't even exercise this level of choice, but let's just stick with the analogy for now.

So is this all real choice or is it something else?

Think for a moment about the democratic political system, which works on the principle of one person one vote. This would seem to indicate that each person has an equal and powerful opportunity to exercise their right to choose which direction the political process takes by voting for which candidate and party they wish to see in power.

Given that there are often very diverse candidates with wide ranging manifestos, this would seem to be a fair and equitable way for power to be divested to those candidates and parties.

However, the reality is something quite different, for the minor parties are never going to achieve power because they have too specialised or narrow a view to ever enable them to win enough of the majority of votes to get elected. Conversely, those parties who genuinely contest the battle for power tend to move towards the centralist or populist areas of the electorate because this is where the election is truly won or lost.

Political parties know that in reality they are only fighting over a few percentage points in the middle, and they therefore compete solely for these swing voters. They try and win these votes by giving these voters the choice that they hope will help to persuade their minds. This appears to be a choice but in reality it isn't, as it only offers a choice in respect of a few minor issues that might tip the balance for enough of those voters that might make the difference between being elected or not.

This is clearly illustrated by the fact that in the UK and the USA, the key issues always seem to come down to character attacks on the opponent rather than discussing key issues of importance for society as a whole.

For example, think how much time during the last election was spent discussing key issues such as climate change, world energy consumption, global poverty and hunger, Aids, debt relief, the unequal distribution of resources, and so on.

Very little.

The parties know that these issues are a hot potato, and they therefore agree not to debate them, partly because they are too controversial, and also because they are in fact insoluble within the current political framework.

So they have no choice but to ignore them.

Also the parties have to be careful that they do not alienate big business in addressing such issues, because if they do then a tremendous amount of lobbying support and finance will be lost.

Therefore the choices on offer are narrowed down to a very small sliver of truth that mostly has not much to do with anything real or deep. In this people think that they can make a real difference by exercising a choice, but the change on offer is a small change within a small reality.

Considering all these multiple choices can keep a person busy on the road to nowhere. For choice is a very different concept to that of free will, as the latter implies a destiny possibility beyond the carnal life of picking and choosing day by day as a means of getting by.

This then poses the question: can a person choose their destiny, and can a destiny choose them?

This is where the illusion of choice can begin to fade whilst the reality of what the truth of life can and might be can really start to bite.

Tony Kearney

Between the shadow and the chimera lies the shaft of light that the truth always represents. Stand in the light, if just for a moment, and see, sense and feel the shadow and the chimera disappear from your eyes. It blinds you not, therefore why should you blind yourself?

The Illusion of Difference

It is remarkable that men, when they differ
in what they think considerable,
are apt to differ in almost everything else.
Their difference begets contradiction;
contradiction begets heat; heat begets anger;
heat rises into resentment, rage and ill will.

Cato

In all differences consider that both you and
your opponent or enemy are mortal, and that ere
long your very memories will be extinguished.

Aurel

Alongside the illusion of choice is the fact that people are trained to see others as being different.

This is quite easily done for different cultures have different languages, customs, religious practices, art, music, diet, education, and much more.

These external differences seem to indicate that there must also be fundamental differences, and the results of this way of thinking are easy to see, for example, when considering the number of wars that there have been throughout world history.

Yet this simply illustrates a different truth, which is that those who see difference in others are simply based on the outside of themselves. For the reality is that we all share the same existence on this planet.

There is only one planet on which we live.

We are all subject to the generosity and laws of nature insofar as we cannot control those forces to any great or long term degree. There are only finite resources upon which we can rely, and we have to find a sustainable way of living with and sharing those resources otherwise our very survival as a species is threatened.

Accordingly, the illusion of difference is, in fact, a luxury and, in the long run, one that the human race cannot afford to hold. For most of these perceived differences come out of such things as greed, exploitation of resources and divergent fundamentalist religious beliefs.

The concept of ownership, whether it be one of ownership over goods, land and resources, or over the truth itself, is a fundamental misalignment. For who, in truth, really owns a mountain, a river or the sky?

Biodiversity is one of the things that make this planet such a rich and wondrous place, but it is also essential in ensuring that the genetic mix of life is sufficiently broad to ensure that life on Earth can continue. Mankind, however, is threatening this balance due to its materialistic and exploitative way of living, which undermines the very principles by which Mother Nature works.

This ultimate expression of difference lies in the mindset that the human race is different, and superior to, all other forms of organic life on the planet. This is an entrenched dogmatism that finds its way into all aspects of human life, from religious fundamentalism and creationist theories, to science and the development of technologies to obtain short-term gain from forcing nature to provide more than it can replace with long-term negative consequences.

All life comes from the same source.

Therefore, life is life and shares and breathes the same contract and the same gift.

There is no difference, only abandonment of purpose.

With purpose comes hope.

With hope comes a future.

With a future comes unity.

And with unity the illusion of difference disappears into the ether from whence it came in the first place.

It's All About Me!

Be content to seem what you really are.
Marcus Aurelius

It is a false principle, that because we are entirely
occupied with ourselves, we must equally
occupy the thoughts of others.

Hazlitt

One of the major problems that people have in the world today is finding out who and what they really are and what they can become. The reasons for this are multiple, for from an early age people are trained *not* to be themselves but rather to conform to some kind of social acceptance where the needs of the individual are regarded as being subservient to those of society.

However, an even bigger problem occurs when a person decides to embark on some kind of journey of self discovery. For one of the biggest traps in trying to find oneself is to try and find oneself!

Now clearly this is a contradiction that needs some explanation.

What is being said here is that many, if not most, self improvement, self discovery, self empowerment processes seek as their primary focus to make the individual feel good about themselves. They seek to boost confidence and self esteem, and that is no bad thing, in and of itself.

However, the person is often placed at the centre of their own world, and this is a fatal flaw in the process. For placing the individual at the core is like asserting that the Earth is at the centre of the Universe, or that an individual is more important than the society in which they live.

This lack of context can only lead to a confused motive for self improvement and, in turn, leads to a hierarchical set of importances rather than a rounded and integrated one.

Mostly this leads to a different kind of selfishness and a perception that, in order to get ahead and make progress, a person has to place their own motives first and ensure that others don't get in the way or prevent the aspirations sought being attained.

There is no altruism in such ways of going on, and ultimately it can only lead to a sort of spiritual materialism, which is no different to the physical kind. It pursues the personal rather than the truly noble and is based in consumerism rather than seeking to become a better person for and on behalf of something else.

Without such a context the development of one's own skills and abilities have no placement in the bigger picture of things. Such motives are self-authorising, and self-justifying and lack a basic humility and humanity.

This self-deceit will cause a person to always ask themselves the question: "What's in it for me?" rather than: "What is in me for it?"

Much of this self-improvement focus does not consider any aspect of service or contribution to the greater good. Thus the culture of me first, me last, and me again if any is left over.

The shelves of bookstores are literally swamped with self-improvement, motivational guides, and ways to improve a person's personal circumstances and relationships. They all look to be helpful in some shape or form, but in reality they mostly turn the reader or practitioner into some kind of spiritual robot that may seek to attack anything that will prevent them reaching their hard earned enlightenment.

Yet a person cannot develop in isolation from others, because if this goodness is not translated into some kind of act whereby the goodness itself is transferred to others, then it can only become sterile and wasted.

This raises the question of why a person would want to develop themselves in the first place? Although most people would say that it was in order to become a better person, in fact often it is done for self-serving and temporal rather than truly spiritual reasons.

It is very hard to escape the ego and identity in such matters, and these giants of prevention are very clever at tricking the person into believing that they are doing it for truly humanist reasons. In reality they may be doing it entirely for themselves.

Some, of course, will openly admit that they are doing it for self-serving reasons and that they are purely looking for self-benefit out of the process. However, mostly such reasons lead to a lack of true fulfilment because they generally run out of fuel.

It is probably no coincidence that the word IDENTITY anagrams to TINY DIET, and in the long run that is exactly what the identity provides: a seemingly large serving of food that is, in reality, not in the least bit nourishing and full of artificial sweeteners and additives.

Curiously enough IDENTITY also anagrams to ID ENTITY, which alludes to the fact that the identity is a child of the ego and this is what the life builds its reality around.

It can be seen, for example, in the actions of some rock stars who earn mega millions by building this persona of being a great big star and then claiming to want to help to fight world poverty or hunger.

This doesn't mean that they are wrong in seeking to see change in the world, but many of them blatantly use such huge public occasions to further or rekindle their careers.

The thing about the identity is that it has the ability to trick or deceive the person into thinking that they are doing it for genuine reasons when perhaps all is not what it seems.

The same can be said about the politicians whom they seek to influence. For as has been said before, anyone who seeks political power should automatically be excluded from having it, as such desires can only be found in those suffering from megalomania!

The more outer power a person seeks the less inner power they access and thereby release from themselves. The more this happens then the more the person begins to identify with what they *do* rather than with what they *are.* Temporal power is transient and therefore finite. Spiritual power is permanent and, because it is Universal, it is therefore infinite in both its scope and possibility.

Therefore, it actually *is* all about you – it always was. It just depends on who and what you think you are! For you can be local, global or Universal in your connections. The longer range they are the smaller and more humble a person becomes. And yet, by the law of inverse ratios, the smaller they are the more powerful they are.

Multum in Parvo.

Is It Really ALL About Me?

Me, me, **me,** me, me,

me, me, **me,** me, *me,*

me, **me,** me, me,

me, me, **me,** *me,* *me,* *me,*

me, me, Me, me,, **me,** me,

me, *me,* me, **me,** me,

me, me, **me,** me, me,

me, me, **me,** *me,* *me,*

me, *me,* Me, me, **me,**

me, me, *me,* me**,** **me,**

me, *me,* me, **me,**

me, me, *me,* me, **me,**

me, *me,* *me,* **me,** me, Me,

me,. **me,** me, me, *me,* me**,**

me, me, *me,* me, **me,**

me, me, *me,* me, **me,**

me, *me,* *me,* **me,** me,

Me, me, **me,** me, me,

me, me, **me,** me, *me,*

me, **me,** me, me,

me, me, **me,** *me,* *me,* *me,*

me, me, Me, me, **me,** me,

me, *me,* me, **me,** me,

me, me, **me,** me, me,

me, me, **me,** *me,* *me,* *me,*

me, Me, me, **me,** me,

me, *me,* me**,** **me,** me,

me, me, **me,** **me,**

me, *me,* me, **me,** *me,* *me,*

me, **me,** me, Me, me,, **me,**

me, me, *me,* me**,** **me,**

me, *me,* me, **me,** **me,**

me, *me,* me,**me,** *me,* *me,*

me, *me,,me,* Me, me, **me,**

me, me, *me,* me**,** **me,**

me, *me,* me, **me,**

me, me, *me,* me, **me,**

me, *me,* *me,* **me,** me, Me,

me,, **me,** me, me, *me,* me,

me, me, *me,* me, **me,**

me, me, *me,* me, **me,**

me, *me!!!*

Boy, don't you get sick of it after a while when all you can see in everything is yourself?

Stop Trying to Make a Difference

In order to move others deeply we
must deliberately allow
ourselves to be carried away beyond the
bounds of our normal sensibility.

Joseph Conrad

I've come to the conclusion that it's
not really possible to help others.

Paul Cezanne

Have you ever had the feeling that you would like your life to make a difference to humanity during your short time here on this blue ball we call the Earth? Have you ever felt that, indeed, it is part of your destiny to make the very difference that the world may need in order for it to avoid some sort of Armageddon moment?

Well, if you have, then this chapter is bound to pour a large bucket of cold water all over that idea!

For despite all this New Age psychobabble about you being unique and making the difference that only you can make, this chapter asserts that the very problem that needs to be addressed is that there are far too many people who *are* making a difference.

Six and a half billion differences is rather a lot and would make Alexander's gorgon knot seem like a piece of cake to unravel, with or without his hot wired solution to solving the problem.

So instead of trying to make a difference, how about the idea of trying to making a sameness in this world? It seems that people seeing and being different has been the biggest cause of the problems that have assailed the human race throughout its chequered history.

Now this isn't advocating some kind of totalitarian conformity or sheep like behaviour, but it does suggest that mostly when people are trying to be different they are trying to be different in the sense of different *from* rather than different *with*. The sense of different *from* has caused many of the problems of the past, for it creates a platform of fear and suspicion, and this in turn creates a ripe opportunity for escalation into conflict.

When powered, this sense of difference bases its centre of gravity in the fact of difference as a first principle, bypassing the obvious and much more powerful samenesses that exist between the observer and the observed. For example, when two human beings see each other as being different, due to their race, colour or creed, they fail to see that they breathe the same air and that if either of them makes it unbreatheable then they will both die.

Also, being different carries with it the sense of ego, vanity and elitism, and these features inevitably lead to the greatest magnifier of all differences, which is competition. People often think that competition is nearly synonymous with Darwin's concept of Natural Selection – but it isn't. If not checked, competition can completely undermine the Natural Selection process. Unrestrained competition is ultimately an unsustainable process, and the last man standing effect eventually leads to their being no survivors at all.

So this chapter is not in any way trying to suppress the notion of freedom for the individual. In fact it seeks to champion it, but in a slightly different or adjacent way.

For why would anyone want to be different to the things that they want to attract in their life? For example, going around hating things is not really a good way to attract love! Nor will being cruel cause other people to be kind to you. This is a very obvious point to grasp, but getting the point of it and living it is quite another matter.

If the things that a person seeks to attract are of sufficient merit and quality, then surely the natural pedigree of other human beings would also want similar things? If this were so, then there would be no secular or religious schisms in the world, because people's basic fundamentals would be the same.

From that place it would be easier to celebrate and champion difference as a richness, rather than it being a point of conflict. Or at least superficial differences would be able to be managed from the fact that the primary power that exists between people is the power of what they share in common, rather than what divides them.

Lack of co-operation and sharing is clearly a failure to see what people have in common. To fight over things that in truth nobody actually owns is unevolved behaviour and species threatening.

In short, it is very silly.

Difference hasn't worked and is not a good formula for success.

Therefore, it is suggested that a person may like to reformat their thinking where 'seeking to make a difference' is concerned.

Perhaps another inroad into this can be provided by the question: different to what and why? But ultimately this question leads back to the same and even more powerful question: what do you want to be the same as and why? Not *who* do you want to be the same as, for people come and go. However the qualities that they portray need not.

This may sound complicated, but it isn't honest!

If a person is inspired by another, it is not the person they are inspired by, but the qualities that they **don't** possess, but rather that they process.

For what is there to say that you cannot process the very same qualities? There doesn't seem to be any shortage of these qualities available in the world. In fact the problem, if any, appears to be the reverse. The qualities themselves appear to be infinite, and there seems to be far too few people to process them.

The reason for this is that people are too full of processing other less fortunate qualities (for these are less potent) but less discerning as to who and what they will allow to process them. This is a pivotal point in looking at being the same as that which you may want in your life.

To be able to process these better qualities requires things like discipline, standards, training and consistency. It is because of this that some people are seen to be more inspirational than others, and are therefore perceived as being role models for others to follow. It is one thing to want to be like certain things in one's life, yet quite another to actually be like them, because the development required to do so is often more than the person is prepared to undertake.

No one can juggle until they practice and the more some people practice the better they get at it. Others, on the other hand, give up after a few feeble attempts, and others again simply never try.

Those who have become successful in the business of living a purposeful life have simply been better practiced at what it takes to do so, and have probably been prepared to pay the price of what it takes to do so, more than those who have had lesser success.

The key to becoming the same as something lies within the question: what do you want?

When most people answer that question, they usually say that they want all sorts of things from material possessions to world peace. Yet, surprising as it may seem, wanting world peace is still wanting a thing that is outside of oneself and is therefore a 'thing'. As such it is being perceived as something that is different to oneself.

The only way a person can see these things in the world, and thereby see them make the difference that they want, is to actually be the same as these things. How else can something like peace be in the world unless it exists in and through people? They do not somehow appear magically 'over there' to remedy or make better some external situation. They exist because some people have consciously chosen to be embassy and agency for these qualities, and have undertaken the development journey to become a safe house for them.

In this context, making a difference sounds somehow miniscule and even selfish. Why make one difference when one sameness can change everything? Many samenesses can cause an exponential power that can change and unite the world. Many differences divide the world and dissipates the power and the potency of both the individual and the collective.

Some may say that this is all a matter of semantics and nit picking. Well it could be but, on the other hand, it needn't be.

What this chapter seeks to highlight is how context and perception about the truth of one's situation is governing upon how effective a person can be in pursuing what it is that they may want, whatever that may be.

To finish this chapter here is a short exercise that can be repeated at different times, according to how the person is placed in themselves. It is suggested that just before retiring to bed is a good time, but whenever there is time is fine.

Think of five things that you would want to be the same as within yourself, i.e. qualities such as tenacity, courage, warmth, etc.

Then think of where you may have seen these qualities before, such as working in other people or in nature, etc.

Then think of how you would want to process these qualities with, and in the presence of, other people.

Then, actually practice them consciously in as many situations as possible the next day (and of course for longer if you wish).

Finally, at the end of the day review the process in yourself and assess how things have gone, what you have learned from the process, and how you might be able to be a better agency for those things in your next attempt.

It's too late to make a difference – we're all in the same boat on that one!

We all have one thing in common, if we're all stuck in the same boat, and that is that we have each other.

What a great place to start.

Can one person make a difference?

Do not go where the path may lead, go instead
where there is no path and leave a trail.

Ralph Waldo Emerson

Wisdom and penetration are the fruit of experience,
not the lessons of retirement and leisure.
Great necessities call out great virtues.

Abigail Adams

Yes, I know this chapter follows on from the one that says: *Stop Trying to Make a Difference.*

So what? Get over it!

In the world today there is, and has for a long time been, a view that one person can't make a difference to the state of the world. The problems that the human race faces, and the issues that are before them, are too big for one person on their own to make a difference.

This chapter advocates that this view is wrong. Because if a person looks at the trace of world history they will find that the story is filled with people, individuals, who *have* made a difference.

ony Kearney

One therefore has to start from the premise that one person *can* make a difference. In considering the great lives throughout history, one can see that they are people who have taken a position about making their mark. Think about the great painters of the world, the great musicians and composers, the great scientists, the philosopher's and thinkers and many more. All great pioneers in every field of human endeavour.

The difference that they have made is indelible. Their lives influenced other lives long beyond the end of their own. The music of Mozart lives on today. The works of the great religious leaders still influence us today, as do the works of the great artists and humanitarians who have inspired and moved people.

The argument sometimes comes up at this point that those people were somehow different, special, unique, and that if a person is not like them they can't make that kind of difference. Yet for every famous person who has made a difference throughout world history there must be thousands of others who have also made a difference without ever being heard of.

The next consideration is that, not only can each person can make a difference, but that each person *does* make a difference, simply because each life is full of experiences and events that have happened to them. These events and experiences contribute to making world history what it is. A person may not think so but it is true, because every experience influences the world in some large or small way.

It is like the theory of the *Butterfly Wing Effect*. This says that even a butterfly flapping its wings in South America influences the global weather patterns. The

4

difference that it makes may not be measurable, but the compounding knock-on effect can be quite large.

There is an attitude to be found in this, which is to not necessarily look for the massive difference but to look to the quality of the differences a person can make throughout their life. Each person has experiences of events that have:

a. influenced their own lives and changed them and
b. influenced other lives and events, which have in their own way changed the course of history.

It is many small efforts in the same direction that count. Those are the ones that cause the long-term change. Revolution doesn't seem to last. Evolution takes longer but also lasts longer.

Many great lives in history have not been recognised in their own time. Van Gogh for example, only ever sold one painting in his lifetime. Yet, in one sense recognition is not the important feature. The importance lies within the fact of using one's life to try and make a difference, and help make the world a better place for having been here.

There can be no better mark for a person to make than to be able to say with dignity, self-respect and self worth that they left things better than they found them. That is a challenge for all, because if that is what a person has done then that energy cannot be destroyed. That is a law of physics. If that is the energy people have generated in and out from their lives, then that will be carried forward and not erased. It lives on in those in whom it has been instilled and gifted.

The above paragraph and the implications it contains merits perhaps a thousand books and lifetime's work of dedicated commitment and love.

However, perhaps for now, read it again slowly and contemplate what it might mean for you the reader, from the inside to the outside. We spend so much time acquiring information that often we do not assimilate the deeper parts into and out from our core of being.

Take the time, rush ye not, for there are parts of you that need to go slow to get there quicker.

For what a great thing it is to share the richness of life that a person has been party to and to pass that on to those that are younger. They can then grow it themselves in their own garden of life and generate it out into the world for those yet to come.

Nature is very clever in how it spreads its seeds.

Human beings can act in exactly the same way.

A person can sow the seeds of what they want in the world, and later reap the benefits and know that the good deeds already done cannot be destroyed. Such deeds are immortal and wait for those yet to come to pick up and champion them in their own way.

As we sow then so shall we reap.
A truth to remember, a promise to keep.
For love's never shallow, it always runs deep.
To live life with honour where the light never sleeps.

How to Make a Difference

Heaven never helps the man who will not act.
Sophocles

Our deeds determine us, as much
as we determine our deeds.
George Eliot

If a person wishes to make a difference then it depends what they are the same as.

In reality it is not actually the person who makes a difference but what they allow to process through them. Human beings can make a difference according to how they arrange themselves, both individually and collectively, in response to any need that they perceive.

There are as many ways to make a difference as there are people on the planet, for whatever a person does or doesn't do makes a difference in one way or another. One of the most obvious ways that they make a difference is by not making a difference! Abdication of personal responsibility makes a difference in that it leads to others deciding the agenda for change or not, as the case may be.

The process of making a difference actually begins in the thinking patterns of the person, because before they can actually make a difference they have to realise that they:

a. *can* make a difference
b. *want* to make a difference
c. then they can explore *how* to make a difference

Without this awareness a person is disempowered from making any kind of meaningful impact with their life. Yet with it they will see that even the smallest act can have a great influence because of the process that has gone on within it.

There is a curious relationship between sameness and difference when thinking about making a difference. If people are all the same from a lowest common denominator standpoint, then no one can make a difference. If, on the other hand, they are all different from having no commonality of purpose, then there is no cohesion into which any individual difference can have a significant effect.

Children are all taught that the law in physics is that opposites attract and that like forces repel. That may be true at physical level but it reverses at higher energy level. People join groups, clubs, get married and form friendships with those that they feel a sameness or empathy with. This is reflected in the saying that 'birds of a feather flock together.'

In any event, perhaps the positive and negative parts of a magnet aren't opposites as such, but rather adjacent or complementary to each other. If they didn't have something in common, in terms of each having something that the other is attracted to, then they wouldn't stick together. In the same way, men and women are adjacent to each other. They are clearly not exactly the same, but something happens when they are drawn to each other. Each part has something the other needs, and hence the natural sense of attraction.

In looking at making a difference, it depends upon what a person makes themselves attractive to or the same as. People don't actually change things. It is what they allow through them that causes the change. Humans are all agency for forces and influences that can, and do, literally change the world to one degree or another. A degree or part of a degree of change is still a change, no matter how insignificant it might appear to either the person themselves or to others.

The amount of that change depends upon the amperage that a person has and whether or not it manages to combine with other forces causing the same change. For many small efforts in the same direction lead to great change. This was the maxim of Mao Tse Tung, when beginning the Long March of the Communist movement from tiny and seemingly impossible odds, when he said that a journey of a thousand miles begins with the first step.

Diamond cutters also understand this principle very well, for they know that a rough diamond cannot be shaped or cut by one large blow as this will cause the diamond to shatter. They know that they have to make many small vibrating cuts, which seem to have no obvious effect on the diamond. Yet they know from experience that eventually they aggregate resonance of all these tiny cuts will cause the diamond to split along the fissure created. Patience thereby gets its reward.

This point is important for two reasons. Firstly, people often give up just when they are about to break through. What they do not realise is that the resistance is always greatest, the risk the highest, the situation most poised, at this critical point of breakthrough or octave change. When people reach this point they can easily give up on years of effort and abandon the project. What is most needed at this point is faith and perseverance, even though there may appear to be no grounds for this.

This is a perilous time for the person and patience and perseverance are needed. After all, this is what brought Moses down after forty years in the desert when he asked God for water for his people. God told Moses to strike the rock three times and that water would flow. Moses then struck the rock three times and nothing happened. He waited a short time, and then struck the rock again. God then spoke to Moses and said that because he didn't have faith and had struck the rock again that he would not see the promised land. He had failed the test.

Secondly, the world uses this understanding against people individually and collectively, for it hides from people the fact that anything worthwhile takes time and it will stretch their tolerances. Otherwise it wouldn't be a breakthrough.

It is said that it takes only 10% of the effort to do the first 90% of a project, but 90% of the effort to do the final 10%. This is called the 'end game principle,' and most worthy projects fall by the wayside due to the inability to appreciate the mechanics of this process.

This process of agency is analogous to the fact that there are many radio stations all broadcasting on different frequencies. People are all like radio sets which can tune into any station they choose, both individually and collectively. Each person has to choose what they will receive from any particular station or they will pick up nothing more than static (which is what most people do because they don't think that they can make a difference).

People also have a volume control on their radio set. They can leave the volume down really low so that they do not attract too much attention to themselves or they can chose to turn up the volume and let the world hear them. It can be anything from Radio Ego to Radio Evolution.

Some start out with their set tuned to a progressive and generative station, but slowly – if they are not careful to monitor the reception they are receiving – other things hear this signal and try and recruit its power to their purposes. History is littered with examples of people losing the original signal and it then being replaced by another coarser one without them even noticing the change occurring.

Perhaps, most sadly of all, some people do not even switch their radio set on. For them the epitaph can only be that they might just as well not have lived. Another analogy for what happens here is that of wedding gifts that never get used because they are too special, and so they sit in a special cupboard, never getting a chance to do what they were made for.

The lesson here is for a person to find out how to get themselves switched on, otherwise they will never know what is possible, what they can pick up, and what they can beacon out. The only way to do this is to try. As Charlie Drake found out in the song *My Boomerang Won't Come Back*, the first thing a person must do if they want their boomerang to come back is to throw it!

But ... if you're stuck in thinking about HOW to make a difference, here's a day-to-day guide to keep you going for a year...

The Diary of How to Make a Difference in the World

1. Don't kill anyone today.
2. Thank someone for something they have done.
3. Don't drop any litter today.
4. Smile at someone you don't know.
5. Don't join the army today.
6. Eat only organic food today.
7. Don't drive a car today.
8. Give something away.
9. Don't tell any lies today.
10. Be on time for everything you have to do.
11. Don't have sex today and thereby prevent population growth.
12. Drink only water today and be thankful for it.
13. Don't read any newspapers today.
14. Say only kind things today.
15. Don't eat any fast food today.
16. Do a bit more than the bare minimum today.
17. Don't watch any TV today.
18. Write a poem, even if it's only two lines.
19. Don't tell anyone else what to do today.
20. Apologise to someone you owe an apology to.

21. Fast for today.
22. Say a prayer for someone you love, even if you don't believe in God.
23. Tidy up where you live.
24. Throw something away you no longer need.
25. Go somewhere different today as an adventure.
26. Wear something green.
27. Read a book.
28. Compose a new tune in your head.
29. Draw a picture of something/somewhere you like.
30. Don't invade another country.
31. Get up earlier than you have to.
32. Don't kidnap anybody.
33. Do not carry out a suicide attack.
34. Do not torture anyone.
35. Do not invent any weapons of mass destruction.
36. Do not pollute the planet today.
37. Plant something to grow today, either physical or spiritual.
38. Put your underwear on backwards. Live with the uncomfortability!
39. Ask someone today what they love about the Earth.
40. Pick up some litter you didn't drop and put it in a bin.
41. Donate to a worthy cause somewhere, even if it's a few coppers in one of those tins in a shop.
42. Deliberately wear odds socks for a day.
43. Hug a tree.
44. Hug a person.
45. Hug yourself.
46. Don't launch a rocket into outer space today.

47. Do not clone anything today.
48. Wonder how much hope you think is in the Universe.
49. Ask if the Universe might want something from you rather than the other way around.
50. Don't be cynical today.
51. Miss a meal today and imagine someone who needs it as having it.
52. Don't shower or wash today and then imagine not having water at all.
53. Say 'thank you' to what keeps you alive during your sleep.
54. Learn a new word.
55. Walk backwards out of a room.
56. Sit in the dark for 10 minutes.
57. Sit in the light for 10 minutes.
58. Drink a glass of water and try and taste it whilst you drink it.
59. Say 'I don't know' at some point today. Mean it and see what it feels like.
60. Whistle for 5 minutes.
61. Close your eyes for 5 minutes.
62. Laugh.
63. Cry.
64. Sing.
65. Hum.
66. Speak gibberish for 2 minutes.
67. Feel your pulse for 5 minutes.
68. Give someone a chance.
69. Do not claim mineral rights over the Arctic today.
70. Don't chop down any trees today.
71. Be courteous.

72. Tell someone something good about them.

73. Don't tell someone something bad about them.

74. Find something to be glad about.

75. Count how many times the letter O appears on a page of a newspaper or book.

76. Try and wake up one minute before the alarm goes off.

77. Try and guess who is on the phone when it rings.

78. Try and guess the colour of the clothes someone you will meet today will be wearing and try and wear the same.

79. Think about compassion today.

80. Call over the word 'hope' to yourself.

81. Don't do any vivisection today.

82. Have no bitterness about anything today. And for the rest of your life if you like!

83. Eat only uncooked and unprocessed foods today.

84. Don't speak all day.

85. Think about the word 'humanity' today.

86. Don't blame anyone for anything today.

87. Don't judge anyone today.

88. Congratulate someone for something today.

89. Don't swear today.

90. Swear just once today and really make it count! But not at someone else's cost!

91. Thank all your ancestors for giving you your chance.

92. Don't employ children in slave-like conditions today.

93. Don't do any factory farming today.

94. Wonder just how big the Universe is today.

95. Write down 5 things you love.

96. Feel what it is like when you wash your hands with water.
97. Avoid being hit by a meteorite as best you can today.
98. Consciously be aware of your sense of smell today.
99. Do not give a bank loan to someone who cannot afford it.
100. Imagine what superpower you would have if you could choose it today.
101. Breathe just through your nose for 5 minutes.
102. Breathe just through your mouth for 5 minutes.
103. Don't say 'never' all day.
104. Try not to say 'no' all day.
105. Try not to say 'I' all day.
106. Eat only fruit today.
107. Eat only vegetables today.
108. Don't make any species extinct today.
109. Spend 5 minutes looking at your hands.
110. Write someone a card or a letter using a pen.
111. Doodle for 5 minutes.
112. Make up a new word with definition.
113. Don't borrow any money from the World Bank today.
114. Don't declare a trade embargo on any countries today.
115. Slowly count to 60 and wonder how many children have died in the world during that minute.
116. Slowly count to 60 and wonder how many children have been born in the world during that minute.
117. Help save the whales by not killing one today.

118. Do not destroy any of the Amazonian Rain Forest today.

119. Other than flatulence, try to make no CO2 emissions today – and try and keep the flatulence down as much as you can!

120. Smile at least 20 times today, it saves energy as it uses less muscles than frowning.

121. Unlike China, don't open a new coalmine this week.

122. Have a really good idea today.

123. Splash water on your face and try and not get wet! Why is water 'wet' anyway?

124. Ring someone you know without any reason other than you just wanted to say 'hi' and wish them well.

125. Write the alphabet backwards.

126. Pick a 'good' word from the dictionary beginning with A and think about it during the day, e.g. 'acceptance'.

127. Pick a 'good' word from the dictionary beginning with B and think about it during the day.

128. Pick a 'good' word from the dictionary beginning with C and think about it during the day.

129. Pick a 'good' word from the dictionary beginning with D and think about it during the day.

130. Pick a 'good' word from the dictionary beginning with E and think about it during the day.

131. Pick a 'good' word from the dictionary beginning with F and think about it during the day.

132. Pick a 'good' word from the dictionary beginning with G and think about it during the day.

133. Pick a 'good' word from the dictionary beginning with H and think about it during the day.

134. Pick a 'good' word from the dictionary beginning with I and think about it during the day.

135. Pick a 'good' word from the dictionary beginning with J and think about it during the day.

136. Pick a 'good' word from the dictionary beginning with K and think about it during the day.

137. Pick a 'good' word from the dictionary beginning with L and think about it during the day.

138. Pick a 'good' word from the dictionary beginning with M and think about it during the day.

139. Pick a 'good' word from the dictionary beginning with N and think about it during the day.

140. Pick a 'good' word from the dictionary beginning with O and think about it during the day.

141. Pick a 'good' word from the dictionary beginning with P and think about it during the day.

142. Pick a 'good' word from the dictionary beginning with Q and think about it during the day.

143. Pick a 'good' word from the dictionary beginning with R and think about it during the day.

144. Pick a 'good' word from the dictionary beginning with S and think about it during the day.

145. Pick a 'good' word from the dictionary beginning with T and think about it during the day.

146. Pick a 'good' word from the dictionary beginning with U and think about it during the day.

147. Pick a 'good' word from the dictionary beginning with V and think about it during the day.

148. Pick a 'good' word from the dictionary beginning with W and think about it during the day.

149. Pick a 'good' word from the dictionary beginning with X and think about it during the day.
150. Pick a 'good' word from the dictionary beginning with Y and think about it during the day.
151. Pick a 'good' word from the dictionary beginning with Z and think about it during the day.
152. Have a good news day – a day when you only tell people good things.
153. Try and say 'yes' a lot today.
154. Really chew your food today.
155. Try listening with your left ear and then your right ear to see if it's different.
156. Try looking with your right eye and then your left eye to see if it's different.
157. Think of someone you know and try and get them to ring you up.
158. Don't use anything electrical today.
159. Don't look in the mirror all day.
160. Pick three words to describe how you feel and then see why.
161. Pick three words you want to be and then think how to become it.
162. Try not to say antidisestablishmentarianism all day.
163. Tidy up where you live today.
164. Do not rob anyone today.
165. Declare where you live a demilitarised zone today.
166. Don't sack anyone from their job today.
167. Don't hijack anything today.
168. Don't spit all day.
169. Be glad of other people's successes.
170. Don't be jealous all day.

171. Don't spend any money today. Be free!
172. Don't repossess anyone's home all day.
173. Clean your teeth with your other hand.
174. Walk slower than your usual speed today.
175. Wake up and count your fingers and toes to make sure they are all still there.
176. Imagine living in another country.
177. Imagine living in another age.
178. Imagine what it is like being the other gender.
179. Imagine being your favourite animal.
180. Imagine being blind.
181. Imagine being deaf.
182. Imagine being dumb.
183. Imagine having a different name, what one would you choose?
184. What one thing would you do today if you could to make the world a better place?
185. Imagine a world without war.
186. Imagine a world without hate.
187. Imagine a world without greed.
188. Imagine a world without poverty.
189. Imagine a world without pollution.
190. Imagine a world without waste.
191. Imagine a world without money.
192. Imagine a world of belonging and inclusion.
193. Imagine a world without prejudice.
194. Imagine a world without fear.
195. Imagine a world with respect.
196. Imagine a world of trust.
197. Imagine a world of co-operation.
198. Imagine a world without politics.
199. Imagine a world without anyone else but you.

200. Imagine a world as if today was to be the last day.
201. Imagine the last thing you would want to say.
202. Imagine the last thing you would want to do.
203. Feel the breeze on your face.
204. Say 'thank you' to the stars. After all you came from there.
205. Radiate peace into the world for 5 minutes.
206. Forgive someone who has wronged you in the past.
207. Forgive yourself for a wrong you have done.
208. Try not to mind that life isn't perfect.
209. Don't blame God for anything today, even if you don't believe God exists!
210. Say thank you to your kidneys.
211. Say thank you to your heart that beats over 100,000 times a day.
212. Say thank you to your lungs.
213. Say thank you to your legs.
214. Say thank you to your arms.
215. Say thank you to your spleen.
216. Say thank you to your stomach.
217. Say thank you to your eyelashes.
218. Say thank you to your fingernails.
219. Say thank you to your hands.
220. Say thank you to your ancestors – all of them!
221. Say thank you to the Sun.
222. Say thank you to the Moon.
223. Say thank you to the sky.
224. Say thank you to gravity.
225. Say thank you to yourself.
226. Don't conduct biological warfare today.
227. Don't build any particle accelerators today.

228. Find something to believe in today.
229. Plan how to be a better person.
230. Don't interrupt anyone today.
231. Count to 100 slowly.
232. What would you want your epitaph to be?
233. Find one thing to change.
234. Find one thing not to change.
235. Walk more on your heels today.
236. Walk more on you toes.
237. Don't use 'um' or 'err' or 'ah' all day.
238. Don't open a zoo today.
239. Act as if you really don't mind what other people think of you.
240. Act as if you don't mind what you think of you!
241. Imagine that you are riding a beam of light through the Universe.
242. Imagine that you are that beam of light.
243. Encourage everyone you meet today.
244. Think of all those who are in prison around the world.
245. Think how much you are in prison yourself.
246. Read a page of a book backwards.
247. Use your knife and fork in opposite hands.
248. Be optimistic all day.
249. Don't hide any nuclear waste around where you live.
250. Look up at the sky.
251. Don't claim to be the new messiah all day!
252. Remember that you are on a planet that spins at 1000 mph. Try not to fall off!
253. Try not to spontaneously combust today.
254. Think what colour love is.

255. Think what colour hope is.
256. Think what colour peace is.
257. Think what colour compassion is.
258. Think what colour faith is.
259. Think what colour belief is.
260. Think what colour the future is.
261. Look at yourself in the mirror for 5 minutes.
262. Try and recall your earliest ever memory.
263. What's the best thing that has ever happened to you?
264. What's the best thing that has never happened to you?
265. Who from history would you most like to have a conversation with? Imagine it happening.
266. Say 'thank' you for oxygen.
267. Wear a patch over one eye and see what that feels like.
268. Wear a patch over the other eye.
269. Write your name backwards.
270. Arrive somewhere you need to go early.
271. Imagine healing force coming out of your eyes.
272. Speak slightly slower than usual.
273. Don't rip anyone off today.
274. Avoid hating anyone today.
275. Try not to have any expectancy today.
276. Give people the benefit of the doubt.
277. Be unconditional.
278. Be a friend.
279. Be realistic.
280. Be idealistic.
281. Harbour no grudges.
282. Seek no revenge.

283. Congratulate someone for something.
284. Try and stop the Sun going down. Humility is a wonderful thing!
285. Try and banish all darkness from the Universe.
286. Try and make the clock go backwards.
287. Try and not get older.
288. Imagine you are 112.
289. Don't think you are better than anyone else.
290. Don't think you are worse than anyone else.
291. Be glad other people exist.
292. Be glad that you exist.
293. Be glad that everything you could ever need exists.
294. Be whole.
295. Be part of the whole.
296. Let the whole be part of you.
297. Keep things simple.
298. Keep going.
299. Keep growing.
300. Keep trying.
301. Don't die today.
302. Don't put anyone down today.
303. Taste freedom.
304. Design a flag for what freedom looks like.
305. Tell someone why you love truth.
306. Ask someone a question.
307. Ask someone to tell you what you are like.
308. Tell someone something good about them.
309. Practise something.
310. Be thorough.
311. Consider whether you think the Universe is intelligent.

312. Consider whether you think the Earth is intelligent.
313. Consider whether you are intelligent.
314. Consider what you think intelligence actually is.
315. What's the best thing you have never thought of?
316. Exercise your body.
317. Exercise your mind.
318. Exercise your soul.
319. Exercise your spirit.
320. Have a stress free day.
321. Don't be political.
322. Don't launder any money today.
323. Look at some money and see just how worthless it really is.
324. Go into a shop and try and buy some kindness.
325. Go into a shop and leave some kindness.
326. Open a door for someone else.
327. Open a door for yourself.
328. Give the future a chance.
329. Challenge your dogmas.
330. Deepen your beliefs.
331. Think something to be better.
332. Write a 7 word principle.
333. Write a personal motto.
334. Count your blessings.
335. Project that no one will be killed by war today.
336. Project that no one will be killed by another person today.
337. Imagine you are a Muslim.
338. Imagine you are a Buddhist.
339. Imagine you are a Christian.
340. Imagine you are a Hindu.

341. Imagine you are a Jew.
342. Imagine you are a Brahmin.
343. Imagine you are all faiths in one.
344. Imagine you are an atheist.
345. Imagine you are God.
346. Imagine you are the other gender.
347. Imagine you were totally stress free.
348. Imagine you have unlimited imagination.
349. Imagine you are the Creator.
350. Imagine you are the created.
351. Imagine you never lived.
352. Imagine you live forever.
353. Imagine there was no greed.
354. Imagine you have all you need.
355. Ask the Universe for something you need.
356. Ask the Universe for something it needs from you.
357. Ask someone else what they might need from you.
358. Watch as the sky doesn't collapse on you.
359. Be thankful if lightning doesn't strike you today.
360. Avoid all tsunamis today.
361. Be glad that the dark doesn't claim you.
362. Wonder why the Universe doesn't punish.
363. Be glad of the Universe's fresh every time attitude.
364. Be moved by the gift of you.
365. Give without counting the cost.
366. And if it is a leap year, be grateful all day for the extra opportunity!

Self-Sabotage

Without adversity a person hardly knows
whether they are honest or not.

Henry Fielding

It has become appallingly obvious that our
technology has exceeded our humanity.

Albert Einstein

In the world today the self-help industry is a massive one, with books, videos, gyms, lifestyle coaches, mentors, food coaches, fashion gurus, Feng Shui consultants, and so much more. This is a multi-billion pound industry full of hope and aspiration to help a person look better, act better and, of course, feel better about themselves.

The main common selling point about all of these is that the person is not where they need to be, and so if they simply follow this diet, go on this assertiveness course or get that Feng Shui advice then suddenly their energy flow or luck will change for the better and all will be well.

What they don't address is the reason why the person may have got themselves into an unfortunate state in the first place. For rather than beginning with the thought that plastic surgery may correct the imperfections a person thinks they have, perhaps it might be more useful to think that most of the damage a person suffers is self-inflicted and probably over a long period of time. It is only when this state of long-term self damage gets to be unbearable that a person seeks to do something about it – and usually they are looking for a short-term fix it cure. They prefer this rather than making a fundamental and constitutional change.

For example, many people today use liposuction in order to lose weight. This is seen as a quick solution to being overweight because it simply sucks out the fatty tissue and no essential organs or muscles are affected in the process. It also means that the person doesn't really have to address the issue of why they may have got fat in the first place, i.e. poor diet, lack of exercise, and so on.

So every now and then all they need do is make a visit to the plastic surgeon and have the unwanted fat removed and all will be well. It might cost a lot of money but it is worth it because the person can still have the best of both worlds, which is to enjoy the pleasures of life and still manage to look good at the same time.

Or so they think.

But really the truth is something quite different. For people mostly believe that it is the pleasures in life that cause a negative result in their health or body image. After all, things like smoking, drinking, chocolate, sugar, fast food, sweets, lack of exercise and so on, are supposedly the pleasures of life, but unfortunately they all seem to have negative side effects.

At least that is the perception and that is why people end up having to take action about the side effects rather than addressing the truth of their addictions – for that is what they really are – and what they cause.

This is why people are mostly unprepared to consider that they are not an unfortunate victim of unfair circumstances, but that they constantly and often consciously self-sabotage in many and varied ways.

Cause and effect is something that people need to face if they are going to get past this self-sabotage psychology. The principal villain in this process is the brain and what it has been trained to think and want. For the human body has a great insight and knowledge of what it needs to function well and how to self-repair within reason.

The human brain is capable of being programmed in many and varied ways and this is something that advertisers know only too well. For all advertising carries a persuasion that somehow, if only they will buy this particular brand of beer or use this perfume or drive this type of car, a person's lifestyle is going to change in a radical and fundamental way.

This, of course, is nonsense and most people know it is – but it still works! This is because most people's brains are more powerful than they are and the brain selects the impressions it likes and then remembers and responds to these stimuli. In this sense people develop addictions to such sources of stimulus or relief because they give a buzz, hit or high. However, this is always a short-term thing and so the person needs to constantly seek reinforcement of this relief to equal out the lows that inevitably come after the highs.

Another problem in addressing this self-sabotage process is that when a person is forced to face reality and take remedial action the cure is often seen as some kind of sacrifice or penitential sentence or punishment. For example, after years of eating junk food and being faced with heart disease a person may be told by their doctor that they will have to change their eating habits or they will kill them. Some people simply refuse to give up and bring on the onset of their demise, whereas others take on board the doctor's advice and begin to eat more healthy food.

But the perception is mostly just that, i.e. that they are giving something up that they like and that gives them pleasure. This, of course, is entirely delusional and self-deceiving for they are not giving up a pleasurable activity at all. They are, in fact, giving up something that has been slowly killing them over a number of years, and hence they need to see that they have in fact been self-sabotaging and now, late in the day, they are trying to stop doing that rather than seeking a cure for their problem.

It is not a case of cure at all, in reality. It is a case of reverting back to more natural behaviour from a place of unnatural behaviour. For eating food that is full of chemicals and additives and sweeteners is not natural. Nor is dieting to try and lose the weight that is gained by eating such food. For, again, the perception is that one is giving up something rather than addressing the self-sabotaging and deciding to revert back to eating a natural and healthy diet. If a person does this they will find that the need to diet will disappear because with natural food eating becomes less compulsive and obsessive because it has less addictive elements in it. Thus natural and unnatural products both have self-reinforcing properties, the former being fortunate and the latter unfortunate in that the chemicals and additives in such foods tend to create cravings, which in turn lead to compulsions and obsessions and thus eating disorders.

Therefore the mindset is crucial in how a person approaches such areas, for mostly people approach them from guilt, shame, low self esteem, lack of confidence, blame, jealousy, and so on. Accordingly, the psychology is usually one of trying to escape from where they are to where they would like to be. This is fundamentally flawed for the person has failed to analyse how and why they ended up where they didn't want to be in the first place.

Again, this often comes down to the fact that they have been self-sabotaging for years and enjoying the short-term benefits, but not enjoying the long-term consequences that it causes. As a coping mechanism a person will usually deny that they themselves are the cause of this result and that they are therefore a victim and someone else had better cure them. And often, because they have left the facing of this self-sabotaging until the last minute, they surrender the healing process to others, often with invasive techniques such as chemotherapy or surgery.

Further, because a person thinks they are being forced to give up something that has given them pleasure, they then regard the so-called cure as like being forced to wear a hair shirt. The cure is perceived as being a process of denial of the thing that gave pleasure and this is why it is doubly difficult for the person to give it up. In truth this is completely wrong, for the thing that gave the so-called pleasure caused the problem in the first place and therefore, in the bigger scheme of things, it can't have caused pleasure at all.

Usually what it does is cause a short-term relief or escape from symptoms that a person is feeling but in fact denying. Therefore, because they do not face and address these symptoms but prefer to escape them and seek temporary relief from them, they compound the problem. This is the classic self-sabotage psychology of hiding from the truth.

Not only do they not address the imbalance, but they also make it worse by taking into themselves a product that masks the pain but doesn't heal it. This has negative long-term impact on the body. It is almost like taking out a mortgage on the body by seeking relief now and paying back double later. This is not a wise move, and if it can possibly be avoided it should be.

All this is not saying that a person shouldn't do any of these activities and suddenly become a hermit or a monk. What it is saying, however, is that a person ought to take responsibility for their actions and not try and deceive themselves as to the consequences of those actions.

Self-deceit is the biggest cause of self-sabotage there is, for this is blowing oneself up in more ways than one. Honesty is always the best policy for it is organic, natural, carries no CO_2 emissions and is unlikely to blow up in a person's face. Rather it keeps a person safe against the needs of the present and the future, and rumour has it that it helps prevent ageing. It is only a rumour, but try it and see if it works!

How to be a Subversive

No problem can be solved from the same level of consciousness that created it.

Albert Einstein

Who does more earnestly long for a change than he who is uneasy in his present circumstances?

Sir Thomas More

Contrary to what the title of this chapter suggests, this section does not advocate becoming an anarchist or a radical reactionary to the current world order. It does, however, propose that a person takes radical steps in their own life, but only in relation to themselves as a first principle and not upon others. The consequences of this taking on of oneself may have a profound affect on others in due course, but only as an overspill of what one has caused in oneself.

The prime approach in this chapter is to canvas the idea that, to one degree or another, a person has become part of the establishment and has adopted behaviours, opinions, views, attitudes and moralities, either directly as a result of the propaganda that they have received in their education, or simply as a reaction to having received this indoctrination. The problem is that the vast majority of information a person receives in their education is usually biased, partial or political, and therefore should always carry a government health warning. The problem is further compounded by the fact that the government is often one of the prime conspirators in compiling this dossier of lies and deceit, along with the media, schools and religions.

All have their views on truth and all have their angles on approaching it and dub in, dub out, edit, sanitise, inflate, deflate, ignore, invent and manipulate reality according to what they want people to believe. This works because people fail to separate the wheat from the chaff where searching for truth is concerned. Accordingly, people often read the papers or watch the news or listen to their teachers or religious leaders to find out what their opinions are.

This is insidious and dangerous, for to abdicate responsibility to others in the search for truth is both irresponsible and negligent. Experience suggests that most purveyors of so-called truth have their own agendas for representing the truth in a particular way to suit their own purposes.

In reality, the truth itself is subversive.

Any greater truth will always look at a lesser truth and see through its charade and see it for what it really is: an attempt to cajole and lure the person into adopting a certain view or mindset that conforms to the norm. Politicians do this all the time by relying heavily on rhetoric rather than substance, for they know that the substance of their argument will often not stand up to scrutiny. Religious leaders do the same by whipping up emotional fervour to cause the flock to stay within the fold, either in the hope that they will be saved or at least be excluded from eternal damnation.

The reason why the truth is subversive is that it challenges the established view of reality, the myths upon which societies base their laws, their social mores and behaviours. These perceptions govern and justify the actions that these societies take, and the so-called leaders massage the truth into the shape that they want it to be and then serve it up to the people as a recipe for how they should think and act.

But truth examines all the ingredients both present and absent and discerns the validity, or otherwise, of the recipe. It does not seek to attack or undermine the canvassed view. It simply seeks to present the correct facts so that people can make informed decisions rather than partial ones. It seeks to give the full context about the situation, and that in turn gives a greater perspective to the decision making process.

The established order always sees this kind of search for truth as being subversive and as an attack on its self-elected right to present the truth as it sees fit. Accordingly it will always attack this approach wherever possible and seek to undermine and discredit it. It argues at the person rather than the issue and will use tactics such as calling the person a traitor or disloyal or a fifth columnist.

By creating this diversion the debate becomes one of the credibility of the source rather than the issue of the truth of the situation. Often this tactic works extremely well and the issue slips out of people's consciousness by being diverted down a side road and parked away quietly until it is forgotten.

Governments and institutions know that mostly they need the support of the people to continue doing what they do. This is why so much misinformation and disinformation is provided to people in the hope that people will become so swamped that they will either agree to the party line or not know what to think or feel powerless to act.

This mostly works a treat because people do think they are powerless.

But people are not powerless at all. What they need to realise is that the real power for change lies in what is right and not in being against what is wrong. For stopping a wrongful action may have its merits, but it doesn't actually put anything better in its place. The real challenge lies in using one's power and will to be the change that one wishes to see in the world, not as an equation of negative things but as a natural response to the premise and purpose of living.

The best way to subvert the many dark and negative forces in the world is to replace them with the forces of love, light and hope. For if one goes round trying to systematically remove all the evil in the world how many lifetimes would that take? Replacing the dark with the light is more efficient and longer lasting.

If it works for the Universe, then the chances are that it will probably work for you as well.

What Do You Want?

Far away there in the sunshine
are my highest aspirations.
I may not reach them, but I can
look up and see their beauty,
believe in them, and try to follow where they lead.

Louisa May Alcott

There are more tears shed over answered prayers
than over unanswered prayers.

Saint Teresa of Avila

This is a very simple question but a very powerful one to start this chapter. In one sense it is the most powerful question a person can ask themselves.

It is almost as though humans are all given a most amazing set of keys with 1000 doors in front of them, and according to what they want do some doors open and others not. All those doors when opened lead to exactly what it is that people say that they want. Some doors lead to a life of greed and temporal pursuits, and others lead to the unknown and mostly untrodden path towards the spiritual purpose of living.

What is important is to recognise that people have a choice to pursue what they want. The first step, therefore, is to realise that there is a choice and that there is a gradient against which that question can be pitched. Anything can be chosen, from perverse and selfish desires to those of spiritual and human race liberation.

If a person doesn't decide what it is that they want for themselves, then there are plenty of other people and things that will happily decide for them. Not only will they decide what a person will do but they will also decide what they think. The list of these influences is long, from parents to teachers to mentors to religious leaders to peer group pressure, and so on.

The answer to what a person wants is constantly demonstrated by what they do. It is easy for a person to speak high-sounding thoughts and principles about what they think sounds good or what they think they should say regarding what they want. However, the proof of the matter is in the doing. It is interesting that the word **DOING** anagrams to **IN GOD**. Perhaps what a person does reveals the God they actually serve?

This does not require a person to suddenly decide to act all holy about life and high things, for that is simply acting. What it means is that a person needs to decide what they personally want from the core of themselves, and out from there letting their actions be governed accordingly. If this is done then there is a far greater purpose and cohesion in the person's life, and also a much greater versatility. The validity of any action is therefore governed not by what is done but by the reason *why* it is done.

Within this there are the inner core or ring decisions as to what a person wants. From that point there are secondary or derivative decisions or wants that are lesser in importance but still part of the process of building the tower of what the person wants and why.

There is also clearly an evolutionary aspect to this wanting process, for the wants of a newly born baby are different to those of an adult. The child's are much more basic and simple, whereas for the adult as it grows the choices and consequences become much more diverse and varied. Yet it is important that people stay in touch with that primal part of themselves so that the decisions they make are from genuine desire and not from a place of should or ought.

It is fascinating to look at the word *desire,* for by anagram it reveals the word *reside.* So, what could be posed here is the question: where does a person's desire reside? In the esoteric core of a person, or in some outer, external, temporary life, which is called the Exoteric? *Exoteric* itself anagrams to *core exit* whereas *esoteric* anagrams to *core site.* This is fascinating because it suggests that in making key decisions about what one wants in a life it is vital to strive to come from the most core place that the person can.

This is the spiritual place of who and what they are and the reason why they are here.

The main reason why humans are here is to find out why they are here and what they are meant to be doing, for something felt it was necessary for the answer to be hidden from them so that they could have some kind of process in seeking to find out why. It is no coincidence that one of the games that children most love to play is hide and seek. Why do they love it so much? Because that is how the natural process of human discovery and enlightenment works. It is not the finding that is the most important part of the game, as that is often an anti-climax, but the actual process of searching. In that process something gets released.

People who are in pursuit of the meaning of life from a more core or esoteric place in themselves are always driven in what they do. They have a great will and desire to learn and find out the meaning of their existence and their part to play in the bigger picture of things. However, alongside this there is usually a great humility and compassion, for somehow they instinctively clue in to the greater will or desire of what made it all. In doing this they begin to sense what *IT* might want, and that inevitably causes a shrinking of the ego and awe and wonder about the magnificence of the Universe, how it works and the greater intelligence at play within it.

It is not possible to want something without being in response to the wants of something else. People's wants and desires are not simply their own, no matter how strongly they believe they are. Humans are vehicles for other things, so in deciding what they want a person equally strongly has to decide what it is they do not want – for one cannot live without the other.

The Buddhist might say that it is the very act of wanting that has got us in to trouble in the first place; that desire is the cause of all pain and suffering. Well, yes and no. It is the aspect of attachment that causes the problems, not the act of wanting things.

Wanting there to be greater compassion, love and humanity in the world needn't have attachment. The same applies to the want to be an agent and embassy for those transcendent qualities to be in the world.

It is not what a person wants that matters, it is the reason why they want it.

So, what do you want and why?

The Feng Shui of You

Only the wisest and stupidest of men never change.
Confucius

The shortest and surest way to live
with honour in the world,
is to be in reality what we would appear to be.

Socrates

In the world today there are many ideas, fads or fashions that seem to have some common feature about them in that they are meant to filter through wisdom from eastern cultures into the west. This is often part of the New Age Movement, whereby supposed ancient principles of knowledge and understanding are meant to provide a panacea for all our modern ills of stressful and dispersed living.

Many of these ancient arts do indeed provide insights and enlightenment into a better quality of life. This includes things such as acupuncture, yoga, herbalism, shiatsu and, one of the more recent discoveries in the West, the Japanese art of Feng Shui.

This ancient Japanese art and/or science works on the premise that all objects process energy and the flow and exchange of such energies can have an enhancing or a negative effect, depending on where they are placed and how they interact with the energies of other objects. Therefore the science involved is one of knowing how to use such forces in a specific way to obtain harmony and natural flow between people and their ecology.

The belief is that everything has an effect, according to where it is placed and how it is used, and this then reflects back into the well being of the person. This would seem to be true, for everyone would prefer to live in pleasant surroundings that give them a sense of warmth, space and freedom, rather than causing stress and anxiety.

Therefore Feng Shui, as a basic principle of external environment affecting human health and well being, seems to be a valid one. The degree and amount to which this is the case can be debated, but the principle appears sound.

If the external features of outside influences affecting the inside ecology are true, what about the converse position, i.e. the inside ecology affecting the outside one? This question therefore leads naturally to ...

The Feng Shui of You

How many moving parts of a person are there which can be arranged in different ways and different combinations to reveal and release different energies and potentialities? There are clearly billions, for this consideration extends far beyond just the physical attributes of the body. Humans are much more complex beings than that, with feelings, emotions, sensitivities, a mind, and much, much more. These systems then all interact to create a dynamic flux of change and balance in every moment of every life.

One of the key elements within Feng Shui is the study of shapes, what they cause and attract, and what they repel. Perhaps this is where people get the notion of questioning what kind of shape a person is in?

States and moods are very complex conditions that reflect how people have arranged themselves, both internally and in response to external influences as well.

The internal state of the person is therefore influenced by multiple factors.

Firstly there are the physical systems of the body. It is often said that we are what we eat, and to a certain degree that is true. If a person just eats junk food it will affect their well being in a serious and negative way. Much of this kind of food is filled with preservatives and chemicals and therefore whilst it may physically fill the person up, there is very little nourishment in it. Further, the body cannot process out these unnatural ingredients, and this is why people who mostly eat this kind of food often end up becoming overweight.

If, on the other hand, a person eats more healthy natural foods, then the body is better able to assimilate the nutriment it needs because it has spent many hundreds of thousands of years evolving to be able to do this. It is only in the last several thousand years that the human race's food base has diversified with the advent of farming and the development of agrarian societies.

For example, although wheat and flour and their products now form a very large part of staple diets all around the world, the fact is that human digestive systems haven't yet developed to be able to process such products properly. This is because, in evolutionary terms, such foods are still very new to the human system. They have only become part of the regular diet since farming technology has been developed, which itself has only occurred in relatively recent times.

This is why many people tested for allergies have intolerance to wheat and dairy products. Wheat is not yet natural as a food to the current human design. When people eat it there are side effects, which whilst not usually immediately damaging can, over time, wear the system down or cause illnesses. This applies in degrees to all sorts of foods that humans eat. The more natural the foods people eat are to their design the better it is for their systems, and the more natural the food is, i.e. the less additives and chemicals, the better it is for them as well.

With this last point there is a serious issue to consider in respect of the relatively recent rise of the chemical industry in respect of the production of food. The benefits that this has yielded in terms of increase in production are, in the short term, massive.

However, this doesn't necessarily mean that the quality of the food has improved. Indeed, there are already signs that the use of chemicals in food production is causing massive strain within various food chains as the land struggles to breathe and find a natural balance due to the exorbitant demands placed upon it.

At some point the land will collapse under the strain because its threshold has been falsely raised due to artificial influences. There is no gain without pain, and as the pressure for greater yields causes the planet's resources to creak under the strain, other short-term solutions with possibly greater long-term problems may be sought.

This is already happening increasingly where the demand for water is now so huge that people are caused to take vast amounts of water from underground aquifers at a rate far in excess of the ability of the Earth to replace it. It takes the planet millions of years to produce this underground water, and yet humans consume it in ever-increasing amounts every year. One side effect of this is that the taking of this water often leaves the ground unstable and prone to collapse, subsidence and even earthquakes.

Even now some people are beginning to re-discover just how sacred water really is, for when something becomes really scarce then it suddenly increases in value. It is curious just how close the words scarce and sacred are.

Food and water are key elements in providing the fundamental platform for the Feng Shui of you. For everyone knows that tap water is not as good as 'natural' water, for tap water is full of chemicals to make it palatable and drinkable.

Here it is important to note that the quality of things depends upon the processes that it has been through.

In recent years there have been a number of stunning books produced regarding this, in particular in relation to water and how it is affected by various processes, from having different types of music played to it to having light shone on it and many other things besides. These processes have been shown to affect the crystalline structure of the water. This in turn suggests that the shape of things determines what they can and do, in fact, hold.

This then raises questions regarding things like Holy Water and how water is used in rituals all around the world. Is it possible for water to be blessed or conditioned in particular ways so that its molecular structure and therefore its properties changed? After all, water is a highly conductive liquid, the proof being that if an electrical appliance is dropped into the bath whilst a person is in it the consequences are human toast in the bath!

It is intriguing that the word *shape* anagrams to *phase*. Could this reveal a hidden meaning, in that the shape of things is merely a current phase that they are going through, and that that phase or shape can be altered or charged in different ways to give the objects themselves different properties?

Perhaps this explains why people who seem to be really good at growing things are said to have green fingers? Is their shape or configuration such that they allow certain energies through themselves that is food for the plants in addition to the physical food the plants receive?

Water itself is a very strange substance. It is a very clever way to safely store two of the most combustible gases known – Hydrogen and Oxygen! It is fascinating that the ratio in which it exists is the sacred one of two parts hydrogen to one part oxygen. This ratio was known to the Egyptians as the Golden Ratio and was used by them in building such objects as the Pyramids.

Next consider the importance of how a person arranges themselves in terms of what attitudes and qualities they receive and process. This links very much to the chapter on thinking, for it is quite a thought to consider that criticism has a shape and so does kindness, hate, compassion, warmth, humanity, envy (which certainly has a frequency for it is said that a person goes 'green with envy'). The same applies with rage, honesty, care, hope, love and so on.

It is said that a square peg can't fit into a round hole. Equally the quality of humanity cannot fit into a person who has arranged themselves in such a way as to be cruel. Or warmth cannot come out from something that is cold, or compassion from someone who is dismissive.

The key to the Feng Shui of a person, therefore, is not that we simply decide to be and act a certain way. Rather we arrange ourselves in such a way that we are attractive to those qualities we wish to attract. We tidy up our affairs if a person we wish to impress is coming round. Why would it be any different with the qualities we seek to impress?

So go on, don't just lie on the couch waiting for something to start. Move the furniture of your mind around and see what might begin to happen.

You become what you think about.
or
You don't become what you don't think about.

One thought fills immensity.
William Blake

Our life is what our thoughts make it.
Marcus Aurelius

The title for this chapter is based partly from the writings of Marcus Aurelius, an early first century AD Roman emperor who was renowned for his wisdom and insight into the human condition. He is particularly remembered for his *Meditations*, in which he espoused his philosophy which came to be called Stoicism. Within his writings are many insights into the notion that a person really does become what they think about.

Thinking is a uniquely human process, and yet it is one of the least understood. For what is thinking? How does it work, and how can it be understood better and thereby be made more effective?

One of the things that is known about the thinking process is that it works by establishing circuits in the brain by engraving or etching patterns in the neural networks. This is like having the internet in a person's head, or maybe more accurately the internet is like a giant brain in terms of its multi-level and multi-dimensional connection possibilities. However, the breadth and depth of the internet systems depend on the strength and ability of the search engine, and of course a person's skill and ability in using it.

This is also true as regards the brain and thinking.

How a person trains their brain, and how they use it, determines just what kind of service they will get out of it. As is known in computer technology, the governing rule is one of RIRO – Rubbish In, Rubbish Out! In other words, it is only possible to get out of a system what one puts into it.

The same principle applies to the brain. It is important to realise and remember that, in evolutionary terms, the massive octave jump in the capacity and ability of the human brain is very recent indeed. Therefore, the brain is like a child and it needs to learn how to behave properly, for if not educated correctly it will run out of control.

People think that it is easy to think because they do it all the time. But is it? For is most of what people do actually thinking or is it something else?

For example: how difficult or easy is it to have an original thought? Reflect for a moment on the fact that each and every person is brought up in particular ways according to their parent's beliefs, the society they are born into, the religion they are adopted into, the education system of their culture, and so on. All these processes etch and condition the thinking processes in ways that make it difficult for a person to actually think for themselves.

The hypothesis here is that the hardest thing in the world is for a person to think for themselves. For when endeavouring to think about any given issue or subject, how sure can a person be that the thoughts they are having are, in actual fact, their own and not something regurgitated from history, a book, TV, school, religious dogma, or some other parochial view acquired from somewhere that they themselves are not even aware of?

Marcus Aurelius knew how difficult it was to actually think. He also knew of the concept that you become what you think about.

The thinking process comes to be conditioned by things like being inducted into a particular religion. This immediately begins to condition a child's thinking processes because, although they can't yet think for themselves, their parents, family and social circle begin to think of them as a Muslim, Jew, Christian, Hindu or whatever. The child is then introduced to patterns of belief and behaviour that are commensurate with the expectations of how they should behave as they begin their journey through life.

This printing process develops circuits within the brain, and as such creates a dominant pattern in the child as to how they think and, more importantly, what they think. Firstly, as to who and what they are, and secondly what they think of everyone and everything else.

This same process applies in respect of what social strata, for example, a person is born into, whether they are a boy or a girl, and so on. In the lower social strata children are often taught to have lesser expectations about their life and their lot, whereas in the higher strata they are taught to have greater expectations about having power, wealth and privilege. The Royal Family are conditioned in their thinking in a very different way to a child born into a family where the parents are on unemployment benefit with no real prospects of getting meaningful employment.

All are conditioned by such seemingly innocuous questions as: 'What do you want to be when you grow up?' The options are tailored and narrowed according to certain expectations and pre-cast judgements as to what is or isn't possible. The author well remembers in his own schooling that the so-called brighter students in the A stream were taught things like science and economics whereas those in the lower streams were geared towards more manual trades like woodwork and metal work. There are, of course, those who do escape this systemisation of their lives, but they are more the exception than the rule.

At a deeper level what is being said is not only, 'what do you want to be when you grow up?' but also more significantly, 'this is *what* you will think when you grow up.' Whilst it is true that adolescents often rebel and react against the views and thoughts of their parents and mentors, the reality is that this response is mostly from within the same paradigm of reality as their parents and mentors.

The next point to consider is that the more a person thinks about something the more they become like it, and the more it conditions their responses and actions. For example, the more a person thinks they want to become a doctor the more they become like one. Then they make the decision to become what they think about, and so they then undertake the six years training to become one. If a person wants to become a doctor then they have to learn how to think like one and that doesn't just relate to strictly medical matters for it pervades the whole of their life.

Then there is the whole minefield of a person escaping what other people think about them, and how worrying about that often influences not only what they think, but how they act. Within this people can develop a whole range of fears and inhibitions that prevent them from being at full and releasing their potential. (An inhibitor is something that is used in electrical circuits to prevent or stem the flow of electrical energy around the circuit.) It is exactly the same for human beings when they themselves, or others, put inhibitions into the thinking system.

The worst offender where this is concerned is the person themselves. For people often tell themselves that they can't do something and then proceed to prove themselves right!

This even applies at individual level where people are even embarrassed on their own when no one else can see or know what they do. This is quite extraordinary for they are probably reacting to what other people *might* think about what it is they are doing. This is not entirely strange for within the thinking processes are such things as memory and linking systems. When faced with particular situations, people's brains and faculties search their systems in a 'where have I seen it before' kind of way. Thus their response can be caused by a link to previous experience, even though the direct cause of that previous experience is no longer present.

Often what happens is that people link to not so pleasant or shutting down experiences. This then suppresses the natural urge to learn and discover. Young children have less of this suppression and this suggests that inhibited response is a learned response. Note: this is distinct from natural caution when facing the unknown, for there are natural instincts within the design that cause humans to have hesitancy when facing unknown and potentially dangerous circumstances.

Thinking, when it becomes established in a particular way, is often very hard to change. As was mentioned earlier, the thinking process is one of engraving, and as something becomes more engraved so the harder it is to change. To illustrate the point, draw a circle on a page with a pen and keep going round and round inside the same circle. The more times a person goes round the harder it is to get the pen out of the set pattern that has been established. Well think of this in terms of fixed mental patternings or processes because the same principles apply.

This is why people and businesses often struggle with breaking out of confined thinking. People are trained and taught to think primarily in fixed ways, and therefore creative thinking is rare because it requires a completely different system of thinking to be at play. It is curious that the word 'brainy' anagrams to 'binary', because the way that the brain is trained is mostly by using a binary system by such things as:

Good/bad
Right/wrong
Success/failure
Yes/no
Reward/punishment
Win/lose
Pass/fail
Pleasure/pain

...and so on.

The more people have experience of this binary system of thinking and linking, the more it prints their mental processes and therefore behaviour.

Here is a story that illustrates the point called the *Five Monkeys*. In a cage are five monkeys and placed in the middle of the cage on a small table is a bunch of bananas. When the monkeys all make a move for the bananas they get sprayed with water from a hose. Each time they try to get the bananas this happens, so they learn not to go for the bananas to avoid getting soaked by the hose every time. One of the original monkeys is then replaced by a new monkey. When this new monkey makes for the bananas he gets attacked by all the other monkeys, although he doesn't know why as there is no spray of water.

Every time he tries he gets attacked again so he learns not to go for the bananas either. Then another original monkey is replaced by a second new monkey and he too goes for the bananas. He is also attacked by the three original monkeys that are left and also by the first new monkey. Even though he has no experience of being sprayed with water, he nevertheless joins in with full alacrity in attacking the new monkey with the original monkeys. Then another original monkey is replaced and the same thing happens again. The two original monkeys and the two new monkeys all join in attacking the new monkey to prevent him going for the bananas. Then the same thing happens again when another original monkey is replaced, the one original monkey and three new monkeys all attacking the new monkey when he goes for the bananas.

Finally the last original monkey is replaced. When a new monkey is introduced the other four monkeys attack it to prevent the new monkey going for the bunch of bananas even though none of them have any experience of the original aversion therapy of being sprayed with water. The new monkey is dismayed and asks why he is being attacked every time he goes after the bananas. To which the longest serving monkey replies, 'That's the way it has always been done around here.'

The moral inside this little story is all pervading throughout people's lives – the 'that's the way it has always been done around here' syndrome. Think how many times a person always puts one shoe on before the other; how they always go the same way to work. How religious services always remain the same; how a person mostly eats at the same time and the same food, just on different days. How the news is always on at the same time, and is always on for the same length of time (is it because there is always exactly the same amount of news that happens every day in the world?); that people always call each other by a certain name, even though they themselves probably didn't choose that name in the first place, and how they print it with what they think about the person every time they speak to them. How school always starts at the same time and bells are rung to start and end class – and also each day's trading on the stock exchange. How people always get paid at the same time of every week or every month, and how they like to celebrate that fact with either a party or showing that they are really free by spending some of it, but then end up short again just before the next pay so they have to scrimp until they get paid. Or how they tend to go on holiday to the same place with the same kind of people as themselves and tend, therefore, to have similar kinds of experiences.

Humans make pasteurised milk look positively dangerous!

How much of this is down to the 'That's the way we have always done it around here' syndrome?

All this makes the story of Pavlov and his dogs seem like a gentle fairy tale compared to what most people's reality looks like. It makes the plot of the film *Groundhog Day* look like a gross understatement of what the truth of the situation actually is. Or for *The Truman Show* - a person could simply swap the name *Truman* for their own. It also makes the Pete Seeger song *Little Boxes* seem very mild against the reality!

As an exercise to assist in this, it is useful for a person to sit down some time with a piece of paper and calculate out of the 168 hours in any given week just how many have been used to do what they want to do simply because they want to. Exclude sleep, work, watching TV for the sake of it, shopping, daydreaming, being bored, doing nothing and see what is left. Hopefully this might come as something of a shock! For in truth there is little quality time available inside people's busy and crowded lives.

Slavery is alive and well. It has simply changed its form to ensure its survival and continuance. That is exactly what all the best viruses do to avoid eradication. If a person doesn't believe this assertion, then they could try and do what the pilgrims did a few hundred years ago, which was to abandon their current life and head off to somewhere like the Holy Land on a pilgrimage. This might have taken them several years, all the time relying on the goodwill of others to see them through.

It's not very likely that the first café a person comes to will give them a free meal simply because they are a pilgrim, and they certainly won't be able to cross the first border between countries without a passport.

One of the tricks that the slavery virus (for that is what it is, in effect) has learnt is to fool people into thinking that they are free when in fact that are not. Just like 'true' slavery the principles governing this process are down to one thing – economics. Slaves are treated like economic units, and still are in many parts of the world, even today.

Yet even the very wealthy can't ever abandon the system because they too have become ensnared by it. Even if they do they still become slave to something else such as money, power or status. Another word for this is addiction. They may think they are in control, but really it is in control of them.

This feature of being an economic unit is easy to see, for once a person's usefulness to the system starts to wane they are either forced out and replaced or retired. The whole system works on the basis of reward and punishment.

Firstly a person has to learn some skills that are needed to survive within the system. Once this has been done these skills are rewarded according to the value system of the culture within which they live. This reward process is through a thing called money, which runs everything. Yet a person can't eat it, drink it, wear it, or do anything practical with it. But try living without it. Today's pilgrim needs passports, travellers cheques, insurance, bits of plastic, a PIN number, a mobile phone, inoculations, and goodness knows what else just to get on the road!

Thus we have the difference between literal and, what is often called, lateral thinking. Literal thinking works in a linear way, whereas lateral thinking encourages 'thinking outside the problem'.

If a person gets outside the problem enough they will find that 'eureka' breakthrough moment where real thinking begins. And that is that there isn't even a problem at all. In fact, there never was one in the first place.

Unlimited opportunity isn't the absence of problems. Problems simply serve – or at least ought to – to show the presence of a greater opportunity.

We lean against that which we resist.

But that which we resist persists.

The point where these two influences meet is in the marriage of being and doing.

As Shakespeare said: 'Nothing is right or wrong of itself, but thinking makes it so.'

We really do become what we think about.

And what we think about becomes us.

A fair exchange if ever there was one.

Self-Leadership

Our remedies oft in ourselves do lie,
which we ascribe to Heaven.

Shakespeare

In order to attain the impossible,
one must attempt the absurd.

Miguel de Cervantes

This chapter looks innocent enough in its title, but the esoteric aspects concern the mask or veil that hides the true reality where the noble art of living is concerned. The fact is that people are brought up inside a world that denies and suppresses true self-leadership and instead subjects all to a dependency way of going on.

This dependency begins from the moment of birth, for a child is totally unable to fend for itself in any way whatsoever, being totally reliant on others to provide for its needs.

Yet the assertion within this chapter is that this natural initial dependency later extends into all areas of human life in a controlling rather than a caring way. People thereby become dependent on a system outside of themselves rather than independent and associated by choice. This is despite the fact that natural human progression and development is towards greater independence and self-reliance first, and co-dependence and mutual reliance second, whereas historically it has always been the other way around.

When looking at the state of the world today and its complicated systems of government, religion and economics, it is clear to see that the trend is towards this state of control and dependency. Perhaps the merits and ills of this trend can best be seen in the world's newest and greatest superpower – the USA. The Declaration of Independence was a marvellous attempt to encapsulate an ideology and theology that placed the emphasis on liberation and empowerment on the individual. At the same time it sought to attribute personal responsibility and accountability on the individual in their relationship with the state rather than impose the state view on the individual.

The idealism of this declaration has never been fully enacted or embodied, yet its aspirations are nevertheless to be lauded as a goal worth striving for. The same could be said of the French model of Liberty, Equality and Fraternity.

In a curious way, from the opposite end of the spectrum, the Communist manifestos have themselves tried to create a platform of communal care and welfare as a means for the individual to progress. Yet all these experiments have failed, to one degree or another, because of external moderating factors, from greed to exploitation to control to power and much else.

In other words, it's very easy to write high ideals. Living up to them is something else altogether. Groucho Marx once said: *"I have principles you know, and if you don't like them I have other ones!"*

The test is therefore not one of being able to quote words on paper, but to be able to be the very thing a person says they believe in by thought and by deed. This is the true test of self-leadership. Anything less than that can only manifest as hypocrisy and as such has the seeds of its own destruction within its constitution.

One of the key ingredients within self-leadership is being able to use one's own systems to think for oneself. This sounds like an easy enough task but, in fact, it is very difficult to do. This is illustrated by the children's tale of *The Emperor's New Clothes.*

This is the story of an Emperor who is deceived into thinking that two tailors are making him a new suit out of the finest silks and gold threads when, in fact, there is nothing there at all. The Emperor, not wishing to look stupid, agrees that the materials look grand, and everyone else who doesn't wish to look silly also agree that the materials are the finest in the land. Finally, on the day of the big parade, the Emperor leads out the parade totally naked. All the people, who are by now victims of the deception, applaud the marvellous new suit that the Emperor is 'wearing.'

All, that is, except one small boy who simply states that the Emperor has got no clothes on. Thus the illusion is shattered and all then agree that the Emperor has, in fact, got no clothes on. The Emperor is then left red faced and embarrassed as all his subjects now laugh at him for being naked in public. Yet this only occurred because one small boy relied on his faculties and senses and simply stated what he saw to be the truth.

This suggests, therefore, that the senses are often overridden by political behaviour, prejudice, opinion or bias. It is truly rare for a person to have an objective thought, and perhaps even thinking that one is an independent thinker is, in itself, very subjective!

Science prides itself on seeking unbiased empirical measurements in its experiments, but the truth is that everything contains a subjective part to it. Even the scientist themselves are part of their own experiment because they designed it. This is becoming more and more evident, even down to the fact that how a scientist thinks about an experiment can actually influence the outcome of it.

This happened recently with experiments into cold fusion where it was found that the scientists who believed the experiment might work got better results than those who denied its possibility. It is an accepted principle now that how a person thinks governs their actions in both a conscious and unconscious way. Thinking is energy, and energy can travel to the source that it is directed to.

This happens at individual level as well. All the time humans are subject to the subjective thoughts of others whilst, of course, the others are subject to their thoughts as well. It is therefore difficult for a person to know themselves and think for themselves when all the time they are being bombarded by everything from news to advertising to political propaganda to religious dogma and goodness knows what else.

Perhaps true self-leadership begins with the realisation and admission that a person probably hasn't been that much of a self-leader. They have, in fact, been more of a follower rather than their own person. Without this admission they may simply not realise the position until it is too late to change.

What, therefore, are some of the key ingredients within self-leadership?

Thinking for oneself.
Taking responsibility for one's actions.
Taking positions about issues that are important in one's life.
Personal Accountability.
Personal integrity and honour.
Not being swayed by the mass of public opinion.
Seeing things through to their conclusion.
Not waiting for someone else to make the first move.
Bravery and having the courage of one's convictions.
Not minding what one meets along the way.

It is much easier to abdicate from all this and simply merge into the crowd and become some kind of sheep and follow the lead of others who are basically elected to think for other people. In many cases they are not even elected – they just do it!

It is often said that people get the kind of government they deserve, and any kind of government based on politics rather than what is natural has to be viewed with a certain amount of suspicion. In politics there are left wing and right wing parties, but in nature one never sees a bird flying with only one wing!

Governments practice control and censorship at many different levels because there would be a breakdown of law and order if they didn't. Yet this is only needed because many people are not able to exercise any reasonable standard of natural government upon themselves. If the choice and consequence process is taken away from the individual, then what kind of deeper collective connection can there actually be?

People are subject to natural laws and government all the time, which both give freedom and form to the natural expression of who and what they are and what they can be. If people were able to practise self-leadership out from these natural alignments then there wouldn't be a need for external governments, taxes, sanctions, wars, money, pollution or politicians.

Yet, like the people in the story of the Emperor's New Clothes, people practice censorship and government over themselves in different ways. This inevitably dulls down their self-leadership skills and abilities.

So, where to make a start where self-leadership is concerned?

Well, it all seems to boil down to one simple question, and that is:

What does a person want?

How a person answers this question reveals much about them. The more material the answer, the less potent it ultimately is, even if they attain worldly riches beyond belief.

It is often said that a person can't take material things with them at death. This suggests that if a person has channelled all their abilities and energies into material things then they fix their life here on this planet.

However, if they choose to pursue a spiritual existence this may then lead them in an entirely different direction where their connections to things are concerned. This doesn't mean that a person should suddenly reject all worldly things, for such a rejection is a denial of the fact that humans live in a carnal world, which they obviously do.

The art is to find the right balance; to find the way to express their potential and possibility by liberating the inner life and not governing down who and what they think they are according to some external criteria.

External criteria always measures results in terms of success or failure.

Internal criteria always measures results in terms of growth and refinement.

Which will you choose to be *your* leader?

Natural Confidence

Confidence in another man's virtue,
is no slight evidence of one's own.

Montaigne

No one can make you feel inferior
without your consent.

Eleanor Roosevelt

This chapter is titled *Natural Confidence*, which is no doubt something that many people would say they would like more of.

It is proposed to start this research from a slightly unusual approach – by looking firstly at what the opposite of Natural Confidence might be.

Unnatural fear would seem to be the antithesis of Natural Confidence and a big hurdle for many people to overcome. Clearly there are some fears that are natural and healthy, such as when being confronted by a wild animal or being threatened by someone with a knife. These fears are normal and natural. They are linked powerfully to the instinct for survival, and there are many systems such as adrenalin, reflex actions, an increase in heart rate, that are the body's natural response to such threats.

There are, however, other fears that are not natural. For example, recent surveys have shown that the number one fear that people have is of public speaking. This is clearly not natural, for all that this involves is a person getting up and speaking in front of others. Yet it is a very real fear for many and it can cause them to freeze, have panic attacks and even be physically sick.

Another great fear is of getting old – yet it happens to everyone. It is an entirely natural process, and therefore to have fear of it suggests that a person is at distance from the reality of the situation and has failed to embrace the processes involved. Of course there are things about growing old that are often difficult, but that is not what is being said here. What is being researched is the fundamental reasoning behind a person's psychology, wherein they fear something they cannot avoid.

The same applies to people who are afraid of dying. Yet this is going to happen to each and every person. To fear such an inevitable and irrefutable truth suggests a deeper fear. It could be that a person is actually scared of erasure and the thought that their life may not have been of great account. This is the fear of there not being any kind of continuance after the physical death.

Those who have lived a full life somehow radiate a sense of settlement and knowing as they approach their death, having perhaps sensed or glimpsed the what next after this life.

Perhaps here the real fear is that of the unknown?

The best place to see natural confidence, rather than unnatural fear, is in nature itself.

One never sees a cheetah chase its prey but then give up because of the censure it may feel from other cheetahs, nor see a salmon give up trying to swim up the river because the one next to it seems to have a better style, or a tree give up growing because others had a head start.

Nature doesn't know how to give less than one hundred percent and will always try its best to maximise its full design possibility. Humans, however, seem to have found ways to sometimes do less than they are capable of. Unsurprisingly this often leads to the erosion of natural confidence.

Consider for a moment the process of a baby being born and how it enters this world. Assuming the baby is fit and healthy, confidence is inherent in all elements of its design, despite how frail and vulnerable it might appear to be. The heart, the lungs, the senses, the reflexes, the nerves, the instinct, and everything else all exude a truly remarkable level of natural confidence. This is encapsulated within the baby's first cry that draws the world's attention to the fact of its arrival onto the stage of human life.

So what then happens to erode this state of natural confidence?

Consider some of the following items:

Competition
Judgement
Criticism
Comparison
Poor self-view
Failure

Rejection
Expectation
Conformity
Censure
Self-censorship

Plus, no doubt, many more aspects about which an entire book could be written… and might be!

What is being said here is that confidence is natural – it is something within the design and faculties by pre-designed blueprint. What actually happens is that, rather than having to acquire it, the truth is that real life experience often educates and trains people away from having it.

In which there are well known expressions such as:

The winner takes it all.
That wasn't very good, was it?
Second place is nowhere.
Can't you be like everyone else?
Just mime the words, will you.
Johnny doesn't seem to have a problem doing that.
I'm afraid you've failed.
You'll never amount to much.
Why can't you be like your brother?
Sorry, you're not good enough for the team.
I don't care, it's past your bedtime.
You'll do it because I'm telling you to do it.
You can't go out until you've finished your homework.
Why? Because I say so, that's why.
Is that the best you can do?

We haven't got all day.

Oh never mind, I'll get someone else to do it.

Plus many, many more that no doubt each person could recite from their own personal history and experience.

It is little wonder that people often develop a lack of confidence when they are bombarded from all directions with such an undermining of their uniqueness and individuality.

What Isn't Natural Confidence?

Some big act of bravado or arrogance isn't natural confidence. It is just bravado and arrogance! This often hides an actual lack of confidence and is mostly an over compensation.

This is what is often presented on things like assertiveness courses with big strong voices saying things like:

Are you sick and tired of being pushed around?

Do you want to assert yourself?

Do you want to take control?

How to unlock the inner you and release your power.

Locating the confident you.

Make that Sale – how to sell yourself.

There's no such thing as no.

Unleash your Potential.

How to get it all.

…and so on.

All this does is replace one act or role with another one because it is dealing with the outer behaviour of the person rather than the core.

In such cases what generally happens is that a weak or submissive person develops an aggressive or pushy style to hide the other role, but no fundamental change has occurred.

Fundamental change happens when a person comes from, and connects to, the fundamental processes of living.

Confidence is clearly one of these processes, for the heart beats confidently over 100,000 times each and every day.

The lungs confidently breathe out CO_2 and take a deep in breath of oxygen.

The Sun confidently beams out the source of almost all the light and heat in the Solar System.

The salmon lacks for no confidence as it seeks to return upstream to the spawning grounds where it itself was born.

Lions aren't known for their shyness as they chase their prey on the savannahs of Africa.

A rooster doesn't seem to suffer from false modesty as it crows in the morning to declare its presence.

Examples of natural confidence are as abundant as there are species on the planet.

Everything that knows what it is has the confidence to be what it is and will seek to do so to their utmost ability.

Except for human beings who have the capacity for self-doubt.

Doubt is the antithesis of confidence.

And the antidote for *DOUBT* is in the word doubt itself, for doubt anagrams to: *BUT DO.*

But do what?

Well, what comes naturally of course!

Such things as:

Enthusiasm
Passion
Trying
Care
Warmth
Genuineness
Compassion
Humility
Value
Tenacity
Awe

They may not be direct links to the building of natural confidence, but then again, they may be!

Why not begin mixing them as a cocktail of life, take a good dram of them and see if they work!

Know Thyself

The Delphic Oracle said I was the
wisest of all the Greeks.
It is because I alone, of all the Greeks,
know that I know nothing.

Socrates

What is not fully understood is not possessed.

Goethe

Perhaps this is the biggest cornerstone within building natural confidence.

This tenet has been key throughout history, for to know thyself at all levels is the most empowering tool of all. Within this comes acceptance of the way the person is, an understanding of the context and meaning of their situation, and a willingness for them to grow and develop to the greatest level that their potential will allow.

People are different and unique and all have natural genius that is special to them alone. No one else has their fingerprint, and therefore no one else can offer the world what they can offer.

One of the great clues in finding natural confidence lies in the fact that it is to be found in looking to a need greater than oneself and wanting to be of service to that need. Natural confidence doesn't exist within a self-serving purpose or goal. It is not an end in itself but part of a process towards being useful to the needs of other things.

Examples in history where people have developed this aura of natural confidence indicate that they have found a mission in life that enables them to develop a true natural confidence about what they are doing and why. Admiral Nelson was a good example of this for he himself suffered from sea sickness all his life. However his bravery, courage, daring and natural confidence exuded a belief and passion that overcame this impediment and transferred to all of his men, sometimes in the face of overwhelming odds.

The Universe is full of confidence, and therefore so is each person. Consider the natural confidence of the Sun as it sends out constant emissions of light and warmth. A person can do that too. Think of the confidence that can be had in the fact that night will follow day and that a person will wake up from their next sleep. There is tremendous natural confidence to be found in the already existing stability of things and their constancy. Then there is the natural confidence in the design when a person simply walks from one place to another. There is also a natural confidence to be found in seeing things work as they should.

Confidence is all around humans all of the time and it lives within them to a massive degree, even if they themselves are not aware of it. The question is, how much is a person connected or not to that web of natural confidence? The difficulty in this being that modern living causes people to be less connected to the reality of permanent truth, and this inevitably causes an undermining of natural confidence.

Some Ways to Build up Natural Confidence

1. See the success that you already are.
2. Build on experiences that give you positive feelings.
3. Give confidence to others – that way you get it back from them.
4. Practise things you feel weak about until you feel stronger about them.
5. Extend your range and versatility as much as possible, e.g. learn a new word every day, read things you might not ordinarily read, learn new skills from carpentry to playing a musical instrument, and so on.
6. Project about how you want to be when meeting difficult situations before you meet them.
7. Count your blessings before you count your problems.
8. Always try and come from purpose and process in your actions rather than perfection and end results.
9. Find ways to improve in what you do and tell yourself that that is what you are doing.
10. Find out what it is that you want from your life and then find out what it will take to get it.

11. Get help and support wherever you can.
12. Surround yourself with things that remind you of what you are trying to achieve and why and that give you positive not negative reinforcement. This includes people!

Most important of all, a person should not allow themselves to be stopped. They should keep growing in their purpose and application into life and realise that there is just so much they are able to give.

A person needs to decide about the core fundamentals and principles about life rather than how good or bad they are at one thing or another. Out from those fundamentals and principles they might then find that these principles also apply throughout nature. Such things as:

Be Natural
Be full
Be economical
Don't waste any opportunity
Fulfil your potential
Share your produce
Invest for the future
Evolve
Grow
Pay back for existence

These overviews serve as a reminder to not mind along the way if everything isn't perfect. Nothing in the Universe is perfect, so why should a person try to be?

Try to create an ecology where natural confidence can grow, and then just find the things that help those seeds grow and flower.

A person shouldn't shrink from what they already are and what they could be, for to do so doesn't do anyone any favours, least of all the person themselves!

After all, things could be worse. A person could have been a rock that was born underground and has yet to see the light of day!

What Do You Represent?

*To practice five things under all circumstances
constitutes perfect virtue; these five are
gravity, generosity of soul, sincerity,
earnestness, and kindness.*

Confucius

To be, or not to be; that is the question.

Shakespeare

This chapter highlights some different ways to think about the above question, and thereby opens up some avenues for further research. It aims to give the reader an opportunity to pause and reflect on how they might wish to proceed in representing the things they believe to be important in their life.

To commence, it is important to think about the fact that we are human beings, for that in itself must represent something. We are not vegetables and nor are we rocks or rabbits. We are human beings, and as such there are many specific and unique frequencies, natures, capabilities and talents within the human design.

Therefore within the design there must be clues that can help locate what it means to be a natural, human representative. What does that design represent, for example, in terms of human race evolution? Because scientists will say that life on this planet has evolved from very primitive organic forms to life as it is today, including the most evolved form yet – the human being.

Humans only use a very limited amount of their capability and talents, and they also have a choice as to how to use them. It is therefore a very important consideration that human beings have the ability to choose what they will represent. It appears that no other organic life on this planet has such a choice – it's fixed. The only choice that other organic life faces, in terms of development opportunity, is whether it can find itself the best possible ecology to fully express its design potential.

For example, consider a seed. It can only develop its potential if it is placed in ground that is receptive to its design feature. It needs the right kind of soil with the right kind of ecology and the right kind of climate in order for it to be able to release the massive potential that lies latent within the seed.

Once, the writer was within the Kauri forests of New Zealand. It is simply breathtaking to see how relatively tiny seeds can develop into these absolutely massive trees. The largest, is called Tane Mahuta, which means Lord of the Forest. When one sees the size of this tree one realises that the Maoris named it well. It is simply awesome to see. Yet if the seed that became Tane Mahuta had originally fallen on barren ground it would never have grown into the mighty Kauri tree that it is.

The other feature within this growth possibility is that, not only does something need the right ecology, it also needs the right amount of space to develop into what its potential represents. Because if there is too much crowding then the Kauri tree can't get to the light and will therefore not grow.

This is the same for human beings. If people can't get to the light of what their potential could be then what they can grow into and represent is going to be lesser than if they have beneficial ecology and possibility. In many ways the possibility of who and what human beings can become is fixed by the world that they live in – the education that they receive, the religious background that they are brought up in, their parents, socio-economic factors, and so on. There are many different things that influence, pressure and change what it is that a person can represent.

When a child is young they are often asked the question: 'What do you want to be when you grow up?' (which for the purposes of this chapter could be interpreted as: 'What do you want to represent?'). This question has mostly limited options in terms of accountant, lawyer, teacher, nurse, or something that is deemed to be socially acceptable. This creates a tremendous pressure on young people because no one really knows at that age what they might want to grow into and represent, for they are yet to discover their own unique pathways and patterns of natural expression.

It is part of the natural expression of each person to find out, discover, learn, catch the way of, what they themselves want to represent, and not what someone else wants them to be. Yet within this, children are herded by their cultural experience into becoming what they *think* they want to represent.

At this point it is interesting to consider the fact of the American political system where there is the House of Representatives. The members of the House of Representatives are voted in on a democratic basis to represent the people. Yet, in reality, there are actually limited aspirations and possibilities as to what those members can represent. Further, it is somewhat ironic for a person to vote for someone else to represent them! Perhaps there is only a need for these kinds of systems of government today because of the lessening of true human natural representative status?

Surely the best representative of any person is themselves, because in a normal circumstance all have the same faculty: sight, two arms, a head, a heart an instinct and many different faculties which humans all share by the fact of having the same basic design.

Yet coupled with this is the extraordinary fact that each person is unique and different. Therefore it suggests that we are all meant to represent subtleties and nuances of expression. This in turn indicates that some incredible engineering went into ensuring that each person is unique. Within this fact alone there is an incredible research opportunity for each person to find out and discover what they themselves want to represent. Because if not, all they can represent is what a lowest common denominator, external persuasion demands from them.

The pressures to conform and simply become 'What do you want to be when you grow up?' are massive. To counter this pressure it is important to pause and consider what it is that a person would want to represent from their life, not necessarily in terms of a title or a position, but in terms of qualities, connections, passions, beliefs, attitudes, stances, hopes and visions.

There are so many things that a life can become because, in presenting oneself open and wanting to be full in the possibility of one's life, the journey of beginning to represent something else begins. In terms of human evolution it is vital to consider what human life represents today, compared to say Neanderthal man.

It is clear that human life today represents something very different to tens of thousands of years ago. On the one hand, the brain capacity has massively expanded in that time, but yet so has human abandonment or misrepresentation of that faculty. One only has to look in terms of how the human race, particularly since the Industrial Revolution, has found ways of misrepresenting itself where the Earth is concerned. What, as an example, does the Industrial Revolution Represent?

It seems to make no sense for such a pristine and amazing human faculty to be applied into finding ways of stripping the planet of its natural resources as fast as possible, as efficiently as possible, in order to make a profit, to make financial gain. That is what it has mostly been used for. Inside that ruthless efficiency not only does the human misrepresent itself to the planet, but it also fails to address the question: 'What do these natural resources represent to the Earth itself.'

Consider what kind of redress in attitude might take place if human beings started to ask themselves questions like: 'What do things represent unto themselves, and what kind of natural response does that call for in terms of respect and value?'

In thinking about what it means to represent something, a clue lies within the word itself, which is to:

Re – present.

This indicates a journey of discovery into what life itself represents. This requires an ongoing research into what life represents, what it could represent, and what it needs to represent.

There is no avoiding the fact that life is a process, and therefore each life is a living process of exchange and embodiment of the very processes that represents. Within human life people make choices as to what they will represent all the time; everything from high religious endeavour to the most appalling and degrading acts possible. The range is absolutely huge, and the choices to be made are just as crucial.

Alongside the above trace about the Industrial Revolution there also needs to be a counter balance representing the positive side of how evolution has moved forward since the time of early humans.

Think for a moment of the great lives in history in terms of what they have brought into this world by the fact of what they themselves have represented from the releasing of their true potential. The great religious leaders and pioneers in terms of religious connection and compassion; the artists who cause spirits to be uplifted; the scientists who help pathfind the way ahead; the philosophers and thinkers who help us consider the nature of our existence; the composers and musicians who give character and expression to higher emotions and feelings that all aspire to; the Samaritans and humanitarians who remind everyone that life is for sharing and giving. Together with many more great people, known and unknown.

In championing what one wants to represent in this world a person becomes like that quality themselves, and thereby becomes greater than just themselves. These are the people that others see as having a presence or charisma.

In wanting to represent something it is vital to consider the whole area of training. As an example, if an athlete wants to represent their country at the Olympics then they need to train in order to compete at that level. They can't just turn up on the day of the Olympic marathon and hope to win it without any training. The same applies if someone wants to be a concert pianist. They can't just sit at the piano and expect to be able to play Beethoven's Moonlight Sonata.

The same principle applies towards developing higher skills and abilities or qualities. This is what the great religious leaders in history did before their missions became public. It has been said that Jesus Christ did much of his training in secret in Egypt before returning to take up the more well known parts of his ministry.

The danger where these things are concerned is that when these people depart others with lesser training then claim to represent what those with higher development stood for. Because of their lesser development, the true message gets misrepresented and warped from the original premise and motive until it becomes something that may be antithetical to the original message.

No matter what the external persuasions and difficulties of any given life in terms of getting by and surviving in this world, within the inner courts of that life, within the indelible parts of the life, there are the options and the choices and decisions to be made. These are to do with what kind of processes and qualities a life would choose to represent.

It really is a representative state of affairs for each and every person, and if this is made more conscious, then the decisions that individuals make out from that representative basis can become much more powerful, both for the person themselves and for humanity as a whole.

There are worse things you can do with your life, but why bother? They are a waste of energy!

What Drives You?

Wisdom, compassion and courage are the three
universally recognized moral qualities of men.

Confucius

Let him that would move the
world first move himself.

Socrates

This chapter begins with considering what drives a car – for a car is a fixed thing. It's made up of a chassis, wheels, steering wheel, boot, windows, an engine, and lots of other parts. But the car itself is inert as it rests with its engine switched off. It can't drive itself. It's got all the parts it needs to be driven but it will sit there forever on its own, unable to move, with a full tank of petrol, pistons, spark-plugs, everything in place until someone gets into it to drive it. Until that happens the car is not going to go anywhere because it's the driver that knows how to turn the key on, put the clutch down, put the car in gear and accelerate away.

The next consideration is one of not *who*, but *what* drives the car?

There are many different types of drivers, and in any given circumstance they may drive the car in a different way. For example, a person might get up in the morning and feel angry because they had an argument and therefore drive aggressively. Or there may be ice on the road and so they may drive extra carefully.

Often the way someone drives a car is reflective of the way that they feel or the way that they are. There are drivers who are very careful and considerate, with some even being over careful and almost paranoid. Then there is the other extreme that drives as though there is no-one else on the road, believing there is no risk and thereby threatening the lives of every other driver on the road.

By analogy it can be seen that when thinking about a human being the very same question could be asked, which is: 'Who, or what, drives you?'

Like the car, the human being can be occupied by something that gets into it and drives, so a person has to decide what kind of driver they are going to be when they get into the car and drive the car of themselves down the road of life. Because, unless they decide what kind of driver they are going to be, then it is a default circumstance whereby whatever is around can get into them and drive them, possibly somewhere they don't want to go!

There are people in life who are motivated and driven for success in the broadest sense of the word. One obvious example of this is people who are driven to make money. There is the story of the man who walked around with a little note in his shirt pocket all the time that said: 'I want to make a million pounds'. Everything he met in his life he referred to that note and asked himself whether that fitted with that purpose. From that premise he would decide what to do.

There are people who are driven to become celebrities, such as people who want to be a film star or be on TV or be famous. These people are often very driven and will stop at nothing to achieve their goal.

Then there are people who are driven to excel, such as those who want to represent their country at the Olympics. Their training programmes are incredible and the disciplines involved are huge to enable the person to achieve their goals of best personal performances, winning gold medals, and so on.

This also applies to concert musicians and singers. These people are driven to practice in order to achieve excellent performance levels, whether it be singing or playing the piano or whatever. It really is a driven thing in people, and sometimes this can even be to the point of obsession.

One example is the story of Marie and Pierre Curie. They were clearly driven in their search for a mystery element that they knew, or believed, existed. This caused them to spend years and years of sometimes soul-destroying work, with no money or facilities, to try and find Radium.

Great explorers are driven by some kind of sense of adventure towards discovering new domains. The sense of the unknown is an irresistible lure for many.

It is clearly possible, therefore, for the human being to be driven by something other than itself. What is important within this is whether a person actually knows when they are being driven by something else and what its nature and purpose might be.

It can be anything at all. It can be greed, apathy, boredom, compassion, care, hate, anger, revenge, peace, healing, kindness, fraternity.

Yet most of the time it seems that the car of the human being is left with the doors open and the keys in the ignition so that anything can get in and drive it.

Perhaps it is wise therefore, to be careful as to what kind of car a person is going to represent – and not only that but what they would allow drive it. Who gets in to that car and drives it is one thing, but it is not only knowing how to drive properly that matters, but also knowing where to go.

That speaks of the need of having an appropriate map that shows not only where the person is heading, but how to get there.

For a flash car that is lost is no more useful than an old banger. Without knowing where you are going it just gets you lost faster!

Spontaneity Training

Life is a series of natural and spontaneous changes.
Don't resist them - that only creates sorrow.
Let reality be reality. Let things flow naturally
forward in whatever way they like.

Lao Tzu

Once we believe in ourselves, we can risk
curiosity, wonder, spontaneous delight,
or any experience that reveals the human spirit.

e. e. cummings

This title sounds like a contradiction in terms, for surely training for spontaneity is antithetical to the whole idea of natural spontaneity?

In truth, it is, but viewed in the context of modern living it can be seen that true natural spontaneity is as rare as spotting a Golden Eagle on the wing in the wild.

People's lives today are highly scheduled and filled with all sorts of demands and requirements. Accordingly it is very difficult for them to simply decide to do something on the spur of the moment because they suddenly feel inspired to and are free at the point to follow through on this urge.

Children are full of natural spontaneity because they live much more by their feelings and instincts and respond in a natural way to their environment and their needs. However, over time these natural responses become more and more over-laid by conditioned responses.

Pavlov demonstrated this response in his famous experiment with dogs when he trained them to link the ringing of a bell with food being presented. After a period of this conditioning process, when he simply rang the bell but presented no food for the dogs, they still salivated because they had learned to link the ringing of the bell with food.

This process applies equally well to human behaviour in many spheres. The classic example of this is the alarm bell going off in the morning to remind the person that they have to go to work. For most people this a groaning experience because they don't want to go to work, but they know they have to because if they don't go to work then they won't get any money and without money they can't afford to live.

Part of the conditioning response regarding this work/life balance is that a person has to agree to work set hours on set days of the week because the work place needs a certain order and guarantee of production levels so that the stability of the business and required levels of output can be met. This means that usually a person has to work a minimum of five days a week and then they can have the weekend off.

However, this means that even on these days off a person's natural spontaneity is suppressed because they have to rest and recover from the exertions of the working week or carry out basic subsistence requirements such as shopping for food and clothes for the week to come.

Occasionally they may arrange to see friends and family but, because of people's crowded and busy lives, this has to been planned ahead to ensure that everyone is available at the same time. As for spontaneously dropping round to see someone on the spur of the moment, well this is usually out of the question and indeed is mostly regarded as rudeness and intrusion these days.

This over organised approach applies at every level of society and is illustrated by the fact that parents have often decided what schools and colleges their children are going to go to before they are even one year old. This is long before the children have had any opportunity to form up their own natural identity and personality, which may turn out to be completely different to the style of education provided by the school they are enrolled with.

The same can be seen with famous opera stars who are often booked up years in advance for specific dates with specific engagements. How can spontaneity find a place in such matters?

The process of this law of diminishing spontaneity can be most easily seen in the forming of personal relationships, and in particular the process of falling in and out of love.

When a couple meet for the first time and develop an attraction for each other then this feeling of spontaneity is present pretty much the whole time. They simply want to be together as much as possible so they don't really mind what they do as long as they are able to be together. So they spontaneously arrange outings, meals or trips together so that they can spend time in each other's company.

Then slowly they decide to commit their futures to each other and perhaps decide to get married. This is what is often called 'settling down', and whilst often this is a meaningful and successful next phase of the relationship, in many others it marks its early signs of decline into role playing, possible boredom and even drifting apart.

With settling down goes planning, planning, and then even more planning.

There are houses to buy, mortgages to get, children to have, and all the rest of it. And as the need for this future planning increasingly encroaches, the celebration of the moment and the whole sense of natural spontaneity become ever more squeezed out of the relationship.

Holidays will have to be planned some time in advance so that both parties can be on holiday at the same time, and they will have to save long and hard because nowadays a holiday means a trip abroad and this can be very expensive. Therefore, the saving for this holiday takes a lot time and effort and this means that there is little cash for other events.

Because of these pressures around money it is very difficult for couples to maintain this natural exuberance and spontaneity. This is largely because they believe that there is a particular type of paradigm that their relationship should conform to, and this leads to them adopting such conformist behaviour in order to 'fit in'.

The more they fit in they more they become fixed, and the more fixed they become the less spontaneous they are.

Finally when they see how the original spark of their relationship has dwindled the less they see they have in common, and often this leads to separation and divorce because they have drifted apart.

This means, therefore, that spontaneity becomes a kind of memory that a person needs to re-educate themselves about; a bit like learning to ride a bike again.

It takes practice to rekindle the spark that a life once had because the alternative is living life in a rut. This is literally true because brain research has shown that when habitual patterns get established this then engraves certain neural pathways in the brain. The more these patterns are followed then the more engraved the behavioural patterns become established. Hence the saying: 'Old habits die hard.'

When this happens the multiple possibilities of brain and neural connections get governed down to a few tried and tested pathways that may, on the one hand, give security and routine, but on the other lead to boredom and apathy.

So spontaneity needs to be practised and planned for. Otherwise how can the unknown of the person find them without the person creating an opportunity for it to do so? One of the greatest fears that people have is of the unknown. This is why most people avoid it and settle for the known. Yet the excitement and discovery of life lives in exploring what hasn't yet been revealed or unlocked.

It is, in fact, easy to find – it's already in the person, inside the spaces between who and what they think they are. There is far more space than matter inside a person and so creating time and space to explore these unknown places can only be exciting and revelatory. Who knows what is in there trying to get out? By giving it a chance you just might find out.

Will

*It takes courage to grow up and
become who you really are.*

e. e. cummings

*Enthusiasm is the yeast that makes
your hopes shine to the stars.
Enthusiasm is the sparkle in your
eyes, the swing in your gait.
The grip of your hand, the irresistible surge of
will and energy to execute your ideas.*

Henry Ford

This small word is very important in looking at what causes people to become who and what they are.

Ultimately a person becomes who and what they want to be even if they claim otherwise. For choice and abdication of choice are equally activating of the processes of becoming who and what the person is in either a positive and life-focusing way or a negative way.

A person either exercises their will over their own situation, thereby influencing the things that come their way, or the things that come a person's way exercise their influence and power over the person. Mostly the case is that the latter scenario is the one that prevails because most people have lives that are based in following rather than leading.

Accordingly most people are subject to the will of other people or situations that they chose to be governed by, rather than taking their own authority from within. This process of surrendering one's own will to that of others takes time but is one that is conditioned into the individual from a very early age by one's parents, teachers and peer groups.

The pressure to conform is huge and stems, in part, from the survival instinct response of herding together to provide some kind of safety. Whilst this has some natural validity at a basic level, at higher levels of response the exercise of will needs to be towards the liberation of the individual in order to allow into the genetic the influx of new and updating influences. Without these new and updating influences stagnation at group and individual level are bound to occur.

The sister of will is discipline, for without discipline will can only exist as a matter of theory. The exercise of one's will has to involve some kind of practical application towards seeing a decision that has been made through to conclusion.

If someone has a will for something to happen there then begins to be revealed the actual disciplines that will be necessary in order for the decision taken to manifest in some kind of form or realisation. Anything other than this can only be intellectual.

As an example, if a person wishes to become adept at any particular activity – from playing the piano to learning to juggle to playing tennis to becoming good at chess – the clear reality is that they need to practice. This requires discipline because a person can't get better at something just because they want to. They have to train hard and develop their skills and abilities in such a way as to be more effective in the execution and application of any tasks they may undertake.

There is the expression, 'where there is a will there is a way,' and this is mostly true. However, often people don't actually find the way they are looking for because they lack the discipline or perseverance to find it.

The reason for this is that mostly people underestimate what it takes to exercise their will to get what they want, and so they reach their threshold of tolerance or discipline point and then give in.

They do this because they want things on their terms, and if this doesn't appear to be possible then they rationalise the circumstances to suit their own lack of will. They then decide that the thing they wanted wasn't that important, or impossible, and so they give up or just don't bother.

This lack of grip is a hard nemesis to escape, particularly because people are trained to have a dependency response to life rather than an independent one. This manifests largely in the fact that a person is trained to believe that they have to do things for someone or something else in order for them to get what they want.

For example, most people work for someone else and this someone else decides what they want the person to do. And if the person does what they are required to do then they get the reward that the controlling person decides that fits.

This dependency state of affairs weakens the will of the person in a major way for they end up applying this principle in most aspects of their life. It can also be seen to apply in matters of religion where people surrender their own will to others who often tell them what to think, and in doing so also condition how they think.

A person is governed in their will by worrying about what will happen to them in the future, both in this life and beyond. This worry leads to fear and fear is a state that is easily controlled by those with a greater will than those of a lesser will. The state and other large institutions have a much greater power base than the individual, therefore they are usually able to easily control the individual's will to such a degree that the person mostly conforms to what they are required to do.

This can be seen in the fact that most people who are born clearly identify themselves as *being* part of a particular kind of ethnic, religious, political, social group that they were born into. They usually confirm this state in themselves for it clearly gives them a sense of identity and belonging. This conformity sense of belonging is mutually reinforced to further thicken the ties between the person and the ecology they find themselves in.

This sense of belonging, or herd instinct, inevitably weakens the individual's sense of will. Often there are conflicting interests as the current order does all it can to reinforce the existing stabilities and status quo whereas the natural interest for the individual is towards finding the unknown, the yet to be discovered, aspects of oneself.

This point of difference is the pivot point known as the *Moment of Will*.

Each person faces this moment at some point in their life, even if they themselves may not ever be conscious of it. The evidence suggests that most people do not face this moment either consciously or in any kind of potent way. They simply go on about their business and exist at the level they do within something else's will, never making deeper or more powerful enquiry or search into what their own actual will might be.

To do so would mean that they would actually have to take control of the steering wheel of their own destiny. Despite the fact that most people would say this is what they want, the truth is that they don't. For the fear of doing so and the possible consequences of such a decision are far more frightening than the suppression of these faculties.

Fear of success is far greater than fear of failure, and that is why so many people do not try.

They do not want to be hurt or fail and therefore cannot love or be free at far greater levels within themselves. These levels exist far beyond personal vanity and power. Rather they relate to a person simply being themselves as they were meant to be.

These places relate to not what a person has in their life but what they are.

If a person wants to be a certain way in their life then that itself is also, and can only ever be, a matter of will.

Finally there is this to say about the process of exercising one's will. Mostly people think that willpower is imposing one's own will over that of another person. There are thousands of assertiveness courses that use this approach as a way of getting a person to 'seize the day' of their life. This is seriously misaligned from reality. For whilst this is mostly how it is perceived and exercised, this is, in fact, a much less potent and effective use of will.

The higher form of willpower lies in exercising one's will over oneself, for in reality the biggest preventer and stopper of the person is the person themselves. The perception that it is other people and external situations that prevent, block and stop the person is, in fact, all part of the misconception and abdication of will that causes the person to misinterpret their situation in the first place. And wrongful perception leads to wrongful action.

A person needs to exercise their will, which comes from their higher faculties of reasoning and logic, over their lower faculties, which are things like habit and comfortability. These lower systems need to be trained to respond to higher command rather than simply ignore it, or as is often the case have no higher command in the first place.

As such this involves training of these lower systems.

An example of this would be simply to get up fifteen minutes before one actually has to so that one can decide what one wants, how one wants to be, and what one wants to achieve from the day.

This simple process means that the person is in control of their day rather than the day being in control of them. As with anything, the more practised a person becomes in anything the more effective they will become at it.

What, therefore, will you do to begin to have more will in what you do and how you live your life? And with this in mind, what is it that you will not do?

You Only See What You Have Trained Your Eyes to See

A fool sees not the same tree that a wise man sees.
William Blake

You may not see the new star in the sky, but I do.
Napoleon

Having spent well over twenty years working as a lawyer and dealing with all sorts of cases involving witness evidence, one thing became clearer than anything else and that is that there is nothing as unreliable as witnesses!

Witnesses are meant to be impartial observers and recorders of fact, but the truth is that nobody sees things without colouring the events, or at least interpreting them in a specific way.

Everyone sees things differently, and they do so for very many reasons.

Sometimes people see things from a completely different angle, and therefore the apparent event occurring in front of them can legitimately look very different. For example, from one angle one witness might think that a person struck another person but from another angle it may look as though the person put their arm up to defend themselves.

Also people will see what they want to see or not, as the case may be. People filter the truth to suit their own particular framework of reality, and this enables them to see things how they want them to be, sometimes flying in the face of logic and reason to do so.

Or on other occasions, they simply dub out or ignore the facts that are presented in front of them so as to justify their actions.

An example of this process occurred when Lord Nelson was planning an attack in the battle of Copenhagen. A signal was sent to his ship by way of flag code from his commander saying that under no circumstances was Nelson to attack. When informed of this message Nelson is reputed to have held the telescope up to his blind eye and looked in the direction of the signal, reporting to his officers that he could see no such thing! Accordingly he passed the order that the fleet was to attack and a victory was won. The rest, as the say, was history.

The main filter of truth, in the case of an observer, is where the person themselves is concerned. People cannot usually face up to the fact that they may be in the wrong, and so they will very often edit the events that have happened in order to show themselves in a more favourable light. This can be done either to show themselves to be not in the wrong or to exaggerate their own importance in respect of positive events.

Very few people are immune from this identity filter, which causes them to see events how they want to see them rather than how they actually are.

As is often said, history is written by the winners, and people like to see themselves as being the winners, or at least show themselves in as positive a light as possible.

An example of this occurred after the Second World War when all the major participants wrote their histories of what had happened. Winston Churchill wrote what came to be regarded as the most definitive work of the War, but true historians now regard his version of events as being coloured by his own craving for recognition and wanting to leave a sense of legacy.

He was reported to have said that history would look kindly upon him because he intended to write it!

He therefore clearly exaggerated his own importance in the dealings he had with Roosevelt and Stalin, for by that time Great Britain was no longer the Superpower it had been. He and the others all knew that.

Nevertheless he sought to portray himself as the key player in the wheeling and dealing that went on at the end of the War as the various parties sought to cement their spheres of influence after the War was over.

Another aspect of seeing what you have trained your eyes to see lies in attention to detail. The highly trained eye can often see what the casual observer fails to notice. This involves a two-stage process, the first part of which is the attention to detail itself. The trained eye dismisses nothing and carefully notes what they actually see.

The second stage is to make deductions from what they see based on a reasoned and reasonable assessment of the facts placed before them.

This forms the basis of all good detective work, for whilst it may involve conjecture or hypothesis it never involves leaping to conclusions for that is pre-emptive and unsafe.

Sherlock Holmes is the archetypal example of someone who uses this method, even if he is a fictional character!

It is possible to train oneself to be better at observation and detection – and what's more it can be fun!

An easy and well-known example of this training is to play the game called '21 objects on a tray'. One person puts twenty-one objects on a tray and the other players get to look at them for one minute. A cloth is then placed over the objects. The players then have another minute to write down a list of as many objects as they can remember. What is fascinating about this game is not so much how many objects a person remembers, but which ones they forget!

Another way to train in this is to simply look in a room for a split second and then leave and try and write down as much as you can remember of what was in the room and where. The first attempts at this are often not very good, but the more a person practises the better they will get.

Also learning poetry or memorising things is useful because it helps forge pathways in the brain that can be used for other things such as recording events when they occur.

Another technique is to use what is called mind-mapping. A person can do this when they have a whole range of issues to consider or think about. What they do is to draw up the issues in small balloons on a piece of paper and then try to join them up so that they relate to and help each other. When developed and practised, this helps to create integrated thought processes rather than fragmented and piecemeal ones.

For example:

Work, family, house, holiday, money, car, mother, schooling for the children, leisure, health, pension, and so on. When thought about individually this can use up quite a lot of energy and this can be dispersing. But try putting them (or a similar set that relate to you) down on a piece of paper in the balloons and gaze at them to see how they relate to each other and how they need to be ordered and prioritised.

Finally there is another aspect of training one's vision, and that is the truly visionary aspect of seeing – looking towards the future and seeing what has not yet happened. This is not as ethereal as it sounds, for whilst the precognitive faculties are an important element of this, they are by no means the only ones.

Reading the trends of things and making sensible predictions about what is likely to happen is a clear and well-practised art. Seeing what is likely to happen and planning accordingly is both sensible and logical. This applies to everything from predicting what the financial markets will do to planning for an approaching hurricane.

It has been said that those who do not study history are doomed to repeat it. Those who, on the other hand, study it and learn its lessons are better prepared to respond to events as they occur rather than being put upon by them.

This is also why some people set trends rather than follow them. They are the pathfinders, the free thinkers, the originals.

It is possible to train one's visionary faculties in different ways. For example, trying to predict who is on the phone or what colours a work colleague may wear that day or what time a family member will walk in the door all exercise and train certain pathways in the brain.

The point is not so much whether the person gets these things right, but rather the very fact of exercising those faculties in preparation for when they will actually be needed for real situations.

The more ready the person, the more ready the response will be.

It's Simply a Case of Mind Over Matter

I imagine that yes is the only living thing.

e. e. cummings

Whether you think that you can, or that you can't,
you are usually right.

Henry Ford

This is a phrase that is very commonly used in the world to indicate that a person can achieve more than they think, simply if they really put their mind to it. But the true meaning and potency of this saying has largely been lost or diluted through familiarity and over use. For what is the mind, how does it work, and how and why can it be more powerful than the physical body?

No one has ever found a mind in an autopsy, a biopsy, or any other kind of opsy one can think of. A mind has never been placed in a test-tube, and no one has yet sold one on Ebay (although they may have lost one on it!), and nor are there any mind transplants available through surgery. This, perhaps, is unfortunate in many cases!

The mind is as elusive as the soul, for it is clearly an unseen part of the human. And yet, despite being the unseen part it is the most powerful. It clearly isn't the brain, for the brain itself is a physical organ that processes information and responses to stimuli. The mind is something that is linked to those processes but it is also so much more, for it has clearly much to do with the translation of that information and the decisions, values and principles that a person develops out from their experiences.

A person is often told to make up their mind, and this suggests that the mind is something that is made up from the multiple experiences that each life has on their journey. From those experiences they need to assess and process the information that they have stored in their brain before deciding what to do.

A mind is much more than just a computer generated fact file that provides information and data sheets from its memory banks. It clearly links to all levels of the person's experiences and draws on those experiences and feelings to decide what course of action is best to take in any given circumstance.

In this sense it is not only the brain that can be programmed to cause a person to behave in certain ways but also the mind. How this works in the brain is quite easy to see for it is used in the education process in a simple and straightforward way. For example, children from an early age are taught that certain behaviour will be rewarded while other behaviour will not be rewarded or even punished. The brain is very quick to pick this up and children learn to conform to the behaviour that is not necessarily natural but expected.

In this humans are like the dogs in Pavlov's experiment where they learn to respond to certain stimuli in certain ways. Many people who seek power and control over others know this only too well and therefore use it to their advantage. The biggest of these tools is fear, for fear creates a state of pliability and suggestibility, and this is a ripe soil for manipulation. Fear of the unknown is the state where a person either looks deeper into themselves to find the resources they need to face the challenges ahead, or it causes them to rely and depend upon others in determining what and how they should think, be and do. Mostly people choose the latter option.

In this way the brain is programmed and the mind is made up from external pressures rather than internal demand. Therefore, the most dangerous weapon on Earth is not a nuclear one but, in fact, the human mind. Although, perhaps, the mind is a nuclear weapon – for *nuclear* itself anagrams to *unclear*. This is what many people are about who they are, what they are, what they really want, what they are capable of, and so much more.

It seems that people who have succeeded in the business of living have been very clear in their mind about what they want and why. This doesn't mean that they have been perfect and not made any mistakes. Quite the reverse is true, for in many ways they have been bolder and more daring and often made more mistakes. However, what it does mean is that they have been literally single-minded and this has enabled them to focus and harness their energies in a much more effective way than Joe Public.

This suggests that having a clear purpose or mission in life is very important in helping a person begin to make up their own mind. This applies in both a positive and negative sense, for even people who are selfish and even evil have to use the same principles to get what they want as people who are both moral and altruistic.

This means that they are driven by a force or power, which in turn creates cohesion and an integration that marks them out as being different to other people. For people are pulled in many different directions by many different demands. This often causes both stress and dispersion. It's as though there is no glue or gel in their core around which something solid can form up because the signal is too weak. This is a bit like Star Trek where Scotty always seemed to be telling Captain Kirk that the gravitational pull was too strong and that he couldn't hold it!

The image is one of the gravitational force of everything else pulling the person away from themselves. A person may underestimate what it takes to make up their own mind because they may not fully realise the unseen forces at play that attempt to resist any person thinking for themselves. Just as the mind itself is an unseen entity, so are the forces that seek to influence it, such as fear, conformity, dependency, institutional behaviour, habit, apathy, guilt, and so on.

For who is immune from the ghosts in the machine that seek control of the driver's wheel from within?

It's Time to think about your Epitaph!

*They are the abstract and brief
chronicles of the time;*

*after your death you were better have a bad epitaph
than their ill report while you live.*

Shakespeare

*Whatsoever that be in us that feels, thinks,
desires and animates, is something celestial,
divine, and consequently, imperishable.*

Aristotle

Perhaps a morbid subject for some but a wise thing to consider now for it helps focus the mind as to both the legacy a person would wish to leave and also what they would need to do in order to crystallise that legacy.

At the end of the day no amount of flowery words or sentiments are going to actually hide the truth of what a person's life has actually amounted to. Therefore it is wise to consider the contribution that a person wishes to make in their life and then set out to achieve the goals set and find the ways and means to do so.

As an epitaph, what is it that a person would wish to be written on their gravestone?

And what do they need to do to be worthy of what is written?

Shock

To be, or not to be: that is the question:
Whether 'tis nobler in the mind to suffer
The slings and arrows of outrageous fortune,
Or to take arms against a sea of troubles,
And by opposing end them? To die: to sleep;
No more; and by a sleep to say we end
The heart-ache and the thousand natural shocks
That flesh is heir to, 'tis a consummation
Devoutly to be wish'd.

Shakespeare

Future shock is the shattering
stress and disorientation

that we induce in individuals by subjecting them
to too much change in too short a time.

Alvin Toffler

Life is full of shocks; some fortunate, some
unfortunate. Some that can be prepared for and some
that can't. Shock is, in fact, a necessary part of living, and
it is the wise person who prepares themselves to be able
to handle shocks when they occur rather than seeking to

avoid them altogether. This does not mean that a person should be on the lookout for and encourage difficulties and obstacles, but rather, when they come, they should be ready to face them with courage and resolve.

Shakespeare spoke of the "thousand natural shocks that flesh is heir to" in Hamlet's famous "To be or not to be…" soliloquy with the sense that by opposing them we may try to end them – but really we can't. They are part and parcel of life and they test and fashion people into who and what they are and what they may become. They are, in fact, levers of opportunity rather than monoliths of prevention.

Shock is a trauma response to some external event that the body cannot immediately deal with. It causes the body to go into shutdown whilst it carries out an assessment of the level of damage or injury caused and what might be needed to rebalance or heal itself. When the trauma is too severe the person does not emerge from the trauma and they either die or enter a permanent vegetative state.

What is interesting about this shock response is that immediately after the trauma event occurs the body goes into emergency response mode, producing chemicals such as endorphins so that the pain felt at the point is minimised as much as possible. This is also why things appear to go into slow motion when such trauma events occur. It is the body, in effect, bracing itself for the shock that is about to happen. Once this initial buffer action wears off then the reality of the event starts to affect the person and they feel the reality of the pain they have suffered and also go into shock.

The principles of this shock response apply to both individuals and groups, for trauma events can affect large groups as well as individuals. Also they not only relate to disaster events but also to events of great success. For shock is usually caused by a sudden and dramatic change of state or circumstance, the two ends of the bar of which are despair and ecstasy. Winning the lottery is as much of a shock as losing a fortune on a financial gamble.

Initially there is the numbing sensation and then the reality begins to sink in, much in the same way as when a baby is born. For a moment the shock of the change of state prevents any noise from coming out of the baby. Then they take a first breath of air into their lungs and out comes their first statement to the world that they have arrived!

The first big shock that a person faces in their life, therefore, is being born. From being safely placed inside its mother's womb, where it is largely insulated from many of the world's shocks, the baby is forcibly ejected into the outer world. There it has to immediately learn how to breathe air otherwise it will die. This is such a trauma that the baby cries with more a sense of shock than pain because everything has suddenly changed.

The baby has been forced into a new octave of its experience and it has to learn how to adapt and cope in order to survive. At the other end of life the person has to learn how to let go of life in this carnal existence before they can enter the next octave of who and what they might become, i.e. physical death. These are the two most powerful experiences a person faces in their time on Earth.

However, in the interim of their life between these two events, each and every person faces a number of shocks along the way whilst they continually try to adjust their direction and steering in order to navigate their way through the sea of life. Some of these shocks are imposed upon the person regardless of their will about them, e.g. puberty or genetically inherited diseases, whilst others occur as a result of and out of a person's own experiences, e.g. falling in love.

Even falling in love is a shock, especially for the first time in the flowering of youth when only a short time before a person may not have been attracted to the opposite gender, and indeed even felt feelings of rejection towards them. But once the onset of puberty occurs then the person's whole system goes into shock with all the chemical, biological, physiological, emotional and hormonal changes that occur.

The person goes into a growth spurt where the physical changes from being a child to becoming an adult usually outstrip the emotional ability of the child to handle them. This is why many cultures have rites of passage ceremonies to try and help the young people adapt to and accept the changes that are happening to them, and also the changes in responsibility that this now calls for. Without this kind of understanding young people can only go into shock and confusion about all the changes that are happening if they don't know why they are occurring or how to think about them.

If a young girl does not know anything about menstruation then when she has her first period she can only be faced with great shock and think that something is badly wrong when she starts to bleed. The same could be said to apply to a boy if he hasn't been told about the process of sexual maturity and the fact that it is normal during puberty for boys to get aroused and feel sexual urges towards the opposite gender.

Sometimes, however, older people make the shock even worse by attaching guilt or shame to some of these processes. This can powerfully print the person as during this time of profound change young people are very impressionable because they are trying to make sense of all that is happening to them. What needs to happen is for them to be informed that the processes are entirely natural and that, wherever possible, they can be aided and assisted to go through these changes safely and carefully. The problem is that being so impressionable this is difficult, especially when they are bombarded from every side with all sorts of information as to how they should think, act and behave.

Such matters only make the already inherent shock within the occurring changes far worse than they need be. For amongst the many chemical, emotional and hormonal changes that are taking place in the person they are also seeking to find a new identity and perception of themselves as no longer being a child but slowly becoming an adult; a person of account in their own regard.

Sometimes the shock of the impending responsibility of adulthood is such that a person can recoil from it, much in the same way as a person recoils from touching a hot kettle. Also some people recoil from the fact of growing older by refusing to age gracefully and do whatever they can to pretend that they are younger than they actually are. The truth is that neither can hide from the reality of the changes that are happening to them. It is therefore wise to embrace the challenges and needs involved with growing up and growing older, as to do so lessens the shock factor.

Further there is a natural vigour and behaviour that belongs to each age, and by preferring and pretending to be in another one a person misses out on the richness that belongs with that age. By doing so people can later come to regret opportunities missed, and this in turn creates its own shock factor.

Events that happen to a person throughout their life are like an earthquake in that there is an initial shock that reverberates throughout the whole of the person. Some shocks are obviously bigger than others, and therefore their effects are more pronounced and longer lasting. Like earthquakes, sometimes these shocks have subsequent tremors that may continue to rumble on for a considerable period afterwards. In fact, some people never get over certain events in their lives and, like buildings in an earthquake, they can be severely damaged or even destroyed. This suggests that the stronger and deeper the foundations a person builds, then the better they will be able to endure the shocks they meet throughout their lives.

Not only that, but they will be prepared to meet them long before the shocks actually occur. For it is well known that animals pick up certain signals about impending disasters and take advance action to ensure that the shock is minimised. For example, in the recent Asian Tsunami it was discovered very few, if any, wild animals were killed in the disaster. This is because they could feel the electromagnetic changes and took necessary evasive action wherever possible to avoid the Tsunami's impact.

This then raises the question about the shocks that might be heading the human race's way, whether we are aware of them and prepared to take the necessary evasive action to prevent or minimise their impact.

People know what many of these shocks are going to be, especially in relation to issues such as climate change, sustainable development, scarcity of resources, economic meltdown, population growth, spread of diseases, and so on. Like the Tsunami when all the water went out to sea before it came rushing back in, everyone has some awareness that a future shock of significant and probably monumental proportions is impending. These recent disasters are something like the pre-shocks before the main attraction.

The difference in this case is that humans can possibly take certain actions to prevent the shock from being as big as it might be if no action is taken. For many, if not most, of the triggers of this impending shock are being contributed to, and even caused by, human behaviour. However, many people, and especially often people in positions of power and wealth, refuse to read the runes of those signs because to do so may threaten their current position of wealth and privilege.

Unless they do so the consequences for them and all involved is that the shock will be more sudden and more catastrophic than they or anyone else could have predicted.

There is a well-known precedent for this effect and that is the story of Noah from the Bible. It is now believed that the story of Noah is, in fact, a later adaptation of an even earlier flood story from Babylonian times, which is probably based on fact. Whatever the case, the moral of the story was clear in that those who did not realise that their behaviour was inviting disaster, and did not listen to the warnings and prepare for what was about to happen, were doomed to be reaped by it.

The parallel with the world's current situation is clear to see, not only in terms of a corollary of a flood due to global warming and rising sea levels, but also the many other compounding circumstances that threaten not only the quality of human life but also its very viability.

Whilst animals may have a more acutely developed sense of hearing or of feeling low, resonant vibrations, humans have, on the other hand, a developed sense of logic and reasoning. The point being that these faculties can predict the logical consequences of certain kinds of activities if they are continued into the future. For humans can run all sorts of scenarios and computer simulations of what will happen if current trends are continued into the future and, in fact, this often happens. And whilst the forces of nature cannot be totally predicted or controlled, human activities, on the other hand, can be regulated to a much greater degree.

However, this depends on what humans regard as being priorities in their so-called standard of living. The problem here is that humans have built a dependency upon a lifestyle that is largely harmful to their own ecology, and as such jeopardises their own long-term future and sustainability. At present many problems caused by this way of life are being avoided by seeking to delay their impact until a future time. This is done by allowing the build up of toxic emissions to remain at dangerous levels, to use sources of energy that are not sustainable, and indeed polluting, or to literally bury the problem (e.g. rubbish, toxic waste) in the ground.

The inevitable consequence of this is that, at some point in the future, the compounding of these behaviours and avoidances will combine into creating a much bigger shock than that which is facing us now. Shortfall compounds the longer the issues are avoided, whereas the sooner they are faced the less the long-term impact will be.

Clearly if the human race is going to face such huge issues in a realistic and meaningful way then some big and uncomfortable decisions are going to have to be made, and at the moment they aren't. This means that the pill that will have to swallowed later will be much bigger than the one that could be taken now in order to rebalance the human race's attitude to the reality of its situation.

Also, it should be noted that the remedy isn't in fact as nasty as it is often portrayed. It is simply that humans have become addicted to a certain way of living and that, like a drug addict, they need to go through a period of cold turkey and detoxification to clean up their act – literally. Once they are through the other side of that process they will see that they are much better off as a result and that their quality of life is much better for the changes that they have made.

The same principles apply also at individual level, in respect of the issues and decisions a person needs to make in their own life, for any crucial issues that are avoided compound in the same way. It is just that the individual's time scales are smaller than the human race's, but the principles are just the same.

Therefore the most effective way to think about these issues of shock is to think long-term as the long cure is always the best. The other important factor is not to be too personal and selfish in making such decisions.

Shock is inherent within the very fact of living but it cannot be fair, reasonable or human to live a life that leaves the human condition in a worse situation than one found it. It is possible to leave things not only as pristine as one found them, but to leave them actually better.

That is a shock that everyone could really do with, which is to be amazed at just how much better things could be if people faced up to the challenges and demands of living in a truly responsible and caring way.

Life's Little Imperfections

*Imperfection clings to a person, and if they wait till
they are brushed off entirely, they would spin for
ever on their axis, advancing nowhere.*

Thomas Carlyle

*A principle is the expression of perfection, and as
imperfect beings like us cannot
practise perfection, we devise
every moment limits of its compromise in practice.*

Gandhi

Following on from the last chapter on shock, here is
a chapter to cause its own shocks.

In case you hadn't noticed, life isn't perfect.

A shock, of course, but pause, take a breath and read
on.

Have you ever thought just how much the Universe
must have got right for you to notice the rather minor
bits that aren't perfect?

Quite an awesome thought, in fact isn't it?

And have you also noticed that most of these bits that aren't perfect somehow relate to *your* personal and somewhat local circumstance?

So, are you the cause or the victim of these imperfections?

Tempting as it is to say that other people are the cause of all that is wrong, the truth is that nobody is that good or powerful!

No, the truth is that people are neither the cause nor the victim of these imperfections.

They are, in fact, here to make them better.

And how do they do that?

By using our imperfections of course! Of which, *in case you hadn't noticed*, you have plenty!

And guess what happens then?

The Universe's imperfections then make our imperfections better at the same time.

When people can learn to love the imperfections of things as much, or even more, than the perfections then they begin to understand what service might really mean.

The greatest urge in the Universe lies within those things that struggle to be higher, because they are the expediters of real change.

So when people look around and see that things may seem more imperfect and lost than ever, don't be fooled.

It is the awakening of the imperfections to two things:

1. Their true pedigree and
2. The subpoena from within and without.

Therefore, having established that things are imperfect, this applies to relationships also.

And here's a turn around thought, in case it fits somewhere: -

Try thinking about the bottom third of all those relationships you hold dear and how to make them stronger, better, warmer, richer, more loving, more human.

The top third is easy - it's perfect!

The bottom third is where the Personal Development lies.

This is what makes some people stand out from the crowd. They don't hide behind their imperfections; they use them as a lever.

Something went to a lot of trouble to make you imperfect. Please don't wreck all the good work and keep those imperfections safe! They are going to be needed like never before.

They believe in what we can be, and they don't mind what we are if we make the effort to try.

Why Not Learn to Play the Synthesiser?

I do not feel obliged to believe that the same God
who has endowed us with sense, reason,
and intellect has intended us to forgo their use.

Galileo Galilei

In nature we never see anything
isolated, but everything in
connection with something else which is before it,
beside it, under it and over it.

Goethe

Most people long to be able to play some kind of musical instrument, and indeed many people can play one or more to varying degrees of accomplishment. To learn how to play any particular instrument to any degree of proficiency usually takes years of training, much like it took the craftsman many hours to make the instrument itself.

Many of these instruments are no longer produced by the single tradesman but are often mass produced, with the exception perhaps of the top of the range instruments where price is not the governing factor. In such circumstances the instrument may still be produced by a master craftsman who takes as long as necessary to produce an instrument of resounding quality that has the human touch and feel that no machine can engender. That is because it contains part of the person who built it.

The same happens in the person learning to play the instrument, for not only do they respond unconsciously to the person and process that went into making it, but they also respond to the influences of the person who teaches them to play it.

From these many influences they synthesise their style and method of playing so that whilst they may draw upon many and varied influences, nevertheless their style will be as individual as their handwriting is.

Years ago, if a person wanted to learn to then play a second instrument they would have to repeat the learning process anew because the new instrument would have different demands and techniques. The learning process of the first instrument might aid and hasten the learning process for the second instrument, especially if they are closely related, but it would still nevertheless take time to master.

As such people who gained mastery over more than one instrument were regarded as particularly gifted, for the discipline needed to master even one instrument was great.

In recent times there has been an incredible amount of technical advancement in the production of musical instruments, and in particular since the rise of the synthesiser. From early and crude models in the 1960's there are now incredibly advanced machines that can produce the sound of a whole orchestra if required. It is often hard to tell the difference between what these machines produce and the real thing. But there is a difference, for one is the real thing and the other isn't.

A synthesiser contains the different prototype sounds of many different instruments. Simply by flicking a switch the player can move from one instrument to a completely different one or a combination of many instruments. Plus they can add lots of special effects to the music by pushing a different set of switches to add any kind of mood or atmosphere.

So whilst the sound might give the impression of being a mini orchestra at play, it is all coming through the one instrument.

In much the same way a human being is a synthesiser of many different forces and influences, for they are all the time absorbing a variety of thoughts, ideas, feelings, experiences, emotions, and storing them in their synthesiser ready for when they might be needed. The player then has to decide which of those influences to incorporate into the tune they may be playing and which ones to leave out. The difference between the musical synthesiser and the human one, however, is that the musical one doesn't actually have all those other instruments in there. It has a computer impression of those instruments whereas the human synthesiser stores actual and real experiences, both natural and unnatural.

However, both can use these stored influences to create any kind of tune or noise simply by pushing the right buttons on their machine. Or sometimes they can let other people push the buttons for them with either useful or disastrous results!

Mostly, however, people play their own synthesiser in a rather hit and miss way so that instead of composing a symphony they create an abstract piece that, at best, has intermittent moments of brightness but mostly is dull, noisy and definitely not catchy or memorable.

This kind of synthesiser produces synthetic music and doesn't feel or sound natural. None of the instruments used sound real because, in fact, they aren't because they are poor quality imitations rather than the real thing. The difference can be noticed quite easily to the trained ear. Plus the more these synthetic influences are blended together the worse it gets as they compound the synthetic and unnatural effect of each other.

On the other hand, the human natural synthesiser – if working well – picks up the true feeling of the energy of the chord they are responding to, and when it plays through them it resonates truly and beautifully. When combined with other natural influences this creates a greater harmony and complementary resonance that is much greater than the sum of the parts.

In such situations there is not the feeling of a synthetic tune but much more one of synergy. For synergy is the combining of two or more energies to create a greater and more mutually enhancing energy than the individual parts on their own can muster.

This is what human beings can and are meant to do in how they live their lives. They are designed to merge and integrate with the great powers and forces of nature, and thereby to make truly great music in the way that the ancients spoke of the 'harmony of the spheres'.

However, because people are mostly preoccupied with other things they don't leave space for these higher influences and as such become more prone to playing synthetic synthesiser music. The proof of this can be seen in the type of music that is popular with young people today, for hardly any of it is tuneful and very little of it is memorable and has more than a very short shelf life. This fact is further confirmed by the lyrics within the songs themselves, which seem mostly to be obsessed with themes like sex, image, violence, greed and alienation.

It is sometimes said that the devil gets all the best tunes, but the best sustaining tunes are those that use the major chords of life, for those are the tunes that have been around the longest and are the most durable. These are the chords that are life-giving and life-sustaining for they warm, inspire and uplift the spirit. They cause people to see that there is a reason and a meaning to their lives and give a sense of inclusion and sharing.

The human synthesiser has been very well designed in order to be able to play all these notes, chords, tunes and symphonies. It is simply a matter of selecting the right notes in the right order. This does need some training in order for a person to become a master but, in actual fact, it takes a lot more effort to play their human synthesiser badly because to do so is not natural and works against the grain of the instrument itself.

With every instrument it pays to have a good teacher, and the best teacher is Nature herself for it constantly and continuously synthesises the multiple forces and influences of her domain. Unless all of it works, none of it works.

Perhaps the Earth, and indeed the Universe itself, could be regarded as being a giant synthesiser with each and every single bit of it having an important part to play in the great key of life.

The key itself to this great tune is timing.

For timing is not the most important thing – it is the only thing that matters.

Attachment and Detachment

Knowledge is proud that it knows so much;
wisdom is humble that it knows no more.

William Cowper

All my possessions for a moment of time.

Elizabeth I

This chapter begins with a journey into space. Most people have seen the situation where one spacecraft links up with another and they dock in space. They are able to connect because of the work that has gone into making them calibrated to ensure that when they dock they fit each other perfectly. This engineering work all took place on Earth, where all the planning and preparation took place before they took off.

Another situation where this docking kind of procedure takes place is in the micro worlds where viruses live. Viruses are many times smaller than bacteria and can only be seen under the magnification of an electron microscope, yet they are very powerful. Viruses work in much the same way as docking space craft for they have a docking part that needs to somehow find a way to lock into the human DNA structure so that not only are they able to live and breed, but they are able to withstand or avoid the attack of the human defence immune system.

This is one of the reasons why the AIDS virus has been so successful because it has been able to bypass the immune system and then replicate itself and then be transferred to another host. Therefore the key to success for a virus is for it to find a way to be attached to its host and then avoid detection by the host's defence systems. It can then replicate and be passed on to other victims.

The first thing that is needed is for the host to have a suitable docking port on which the virus can land and then lock. If it can't do this then it has no chance of surviving. This docking procedure helps explain why some species are prone to certain viruses whereas others are not affected by them at all. This is because that particular virus has evolved and adapted its docking device to match that of its most suitable host.

Sometimes this relationship can be mutually beneficial and at other times it can be parasitic, but the same principle applies in every case.

This same process of docking applies to human behaviour for certain natures and qualities can only land on and dock with a person if they have the portals to allow these influences to do so. In other words, you have to have gold to get gold.

The danger in this is that if a person acts in a certain negative way then they are sending out a signal saying that they are open to receiving more of that kind of virus and becoming a home for it. This means that they become a host for it, and if they are not careful the virus takes them over to such a degree that they cannot do anything to stop it. Like other viruses it can, in the end, kill them. For things like hate, greed, envy, lust and obsession can literally consume a person if they are allowed to take hold and spread.

However, it's not all bad news. Good things also use the same process to become attached to a person and enhance both the person and what they do and who they meet. This is why we often say that someone has a charisma or an aura about them. They literally do because quality radiates an energy field and this can be felt and even sometimes seen. Hence the saying that quality is felt and not portrayed.

It therefore pays to check one's docking system, for the negative attributes use a completely different set of procedures to the positive ones. A bomb can't land on a runway in the same way that a glider can! It also doesn't leave the runway fit for anything else but other bombs to land on it whereas the glider leaves the runway in perfect condition for other aircraft to land after it.

It's Time for a Brainwave

*All the armies in the world cannot defeat an idea
whose time has come.*

Victor Hugo

*It is astonishing what an effort it seems to be for
many people to put their brains
definitely and systematically to work.*

Thomas A. Edison

A brainwave is regarded as being an amazing idea or
revelation; a spark of genius that allows something truly
original to appear. The image that is used to convey this
in picture form is usually one of a light bulb switching
on above the person's head. The sound effect most used
is that of a bell ringing by going 'ding!'

But the original meaning of the word brainwave has
an interesting insight into what a brainwave actually is
and how it works. For it has only been discovered in
relatively recent times that the way the brain receives
and translates information is through a wave pattern of
electrical impressions.

The pioneer of this breakthrough discovery was a man called Hans Berger in Germany in the late 1920's. He managed to prove through experiments that the brain produces electrical impulses or waves and that these can be recorded physically on machines.

His research was sparked by the previous discovery that the heart itself was governed and run by electrical impulses and that these impulses could be measured on an electrocardiogram. Berger wondered if perhaps the brain also ran in a similar way.

After many years of research he finally managed to record these electrical signals in the brain by attaching two electrodes to a person's scalp and then recording the electrical signals that the device picked up. He called this new device an electroencephalogram (EEG), and today these are widely used in helping to assess and diagnose many brain conditions in patients.

The EEG has evolved vastly since Berger's day, and the amount of things known about the brain and how it works has also grown massively. Yet the more that is learnt about the brain and how it works the more mystery there is.

One of the interesting features about the brain is that there are different types of waves that work within it, operating in different ways and causing different things. There are, for example, alpha, beta, delta and theta waves. These are of different wavelengths and, as such, cause different states in the brain and forge different connections within it. These states and connections then affect the behaviour of the person.

The question then arises: does the person's behaviour cause the wave pattern of the brain or do the wave patterns within the brain affect the behaviour of the person? The answer is that both apply in equal measure because the system is one of self-reinforcement.

The brain is a massive neural network and it interprets the information it receives in a cogent and intelligent way in order that the person can respond to the stimulus input.

The problem with this is that the brain can only translate the information it receives according to the breadth of its reference fields and wave patterns that it has established. New information tends to be translated according to old patterns once a certain amount of fixed patterning has been established in the brain.

Initially these fixed patterns are established from outside via a simple pain and pleasure reinforcement methodology. That is to say that 'good' behaviour is rewarded and 'bad' behaviour is not. The brain learns these techniques very quickly and then sets up a circuit whereby these feelings are sought out and reinforced every time they are felt.

This is why feelings of pain and pleasure are described as being sensations. This is literally the case, with the feelings being carried wave-like throughout the body up to the brain. It then translates the feelings felt and sends back signals of either pleasure and enjoyment or pain and aversion.

This helps explain the use of shock aversion therapy where feelings of aversion come to be learnt to be associated with a behavioural pattern that a person wishes to break. Each time the person begins to engage in the behaviour they are given an electric shock. So they learn not to do it any more as the pleasure they originally got from doing the activity has come to be overtaken by the pain of the shock now associated with it.

In time even the thought of the activity causes negative feelings as the person remembers the feeling of the shock and so they no longer need the actual shock treatment as the brain has learnt to associate the thought of the negative behaviour. It then produces a memory feeling of the shock. This in turn causes the person to modify the behavioural pattern in order to prevent the onset of the feeling of pain now intrinsically associated with the behaviour.

The same principle clearly applies to behaviour that gives pleasure, in that a positive neural network is set up. The more this behaviour is carried out the more it becomes reinforced and therefore the easier it is to do. The down side of this is that the more it is done the less of the original sensation there is about it because the brain has learnt to anticipate the feeling and so it doesn't quite have the same buzz about it.

This means that often people have to find ways to spark up the activity in order to get the buzz they require. This can be seen easily in things like adventure activities where people who are, in effect, addicted to adrenalin need to do more and more extreme activities in order to get the high that they seek.

This aspect of the brain working by wave power has been researched quite extensively, and it is known, for example, that during waking hours the brain works more on alpha waves, whereas in deep and relaxing sleep the brain has more delta wave activity. Alpha waves are more short wave, and given the amount of information people are required to assimilate and respond to during the course of a waking day, it is no wonder that the alpha wave frequency rules the brain's airways.

However most of this traffic is mundane, ordinary and repetitive. Because of this fact the brain works at much lower capacity than it is in fact capable of doing. It does, therefore, literally get stuck in a rut because the routine of life is such that a person often knows exactly what they are going to be doing months in advance.

They plan their holidays, weddings, education of their children, and so forth, far ahead simply because they have to otherwise there will be no space and time to carry out these activities when they want to.

Life then is generally a pattern of robotic behavioural patterns, interspersed with the occasional high points, before going back to the regular routine. This habitual pattern becomes self-reinforcing; for the more something is done the harder it is to change. The harder it is to change, the more difficult it is to set up a new wave pattern in the brain – and thereby have a brainwave.

Accordingly, it is vital that a person sets up specific opportunities in their life to enable them to have a much better chance of having a brainwave, or indeed a series of brainwaves.

To do this a person needs to create specific times and places for this to happen. This may seem to be extremely difficult, given the fact that people live such busy and crowded lives, but in fact it isn't. For it is not the amount of time dedicated to such activities that matters but the quality.

This can involve setting aside a specific time every day or week for specific brainwave activities. This doesn't just mean generating lots of different ideas about the future, although that is clearly a part of it. It would include specific times where a person does the complete opposite, which is to completely empty themselves out of all ideas and noise and slow themselves right down, thereby connecting to different wave patterns in the brain.

This would mean times of ideas generation and other times of meditation, for it is clear that the brain works on different wavelengths and all are needed to be in good working order to allow the brain to work at greater capacity. It is often said that the brain rarely works at more than 10% of its capacity. In order for it to work more efficiently more effective methods for its use need to be developed.

This means setting up new neural networks, for the ordinary everyday ones do not lead to what we know as brainwaves. To facilitate this, a person needs to be able to think outside the box of their usual conformity patterns.

This requires ingenuity, for the brain has the ability to quickly turn things into formulas. So the brain needs to be constantly surprised and kept interested so that new and bright brain waves can be induced. On the other hand, it also needs to be trained to slow down when life gets too hectic and too dispersed.

The important thing to note about the brain is that unless it is trained and controlled it will think that it is in charge of the person and cause them to do things that it likes, rather than what the person might actually need to do. The brain doesn't actually mind what it does as long as it is given precise instructions as to what is required of it. If this doesn't happen then it gets bored and either shuts down and becomes atrophied or seeks titillation and excitement to relieve the boredom.

Therefore to train the brain it is necessary to both instruct it and keep it interested in the activities being pursued. This, in fact, should not be difficult, providing the brain itself sees that there is some reward for it in engaging in these processes of mind and consciousness expansion.

With over a billion, billion possible connections in the brain, and an infinite Universe to contemplate, that shouldn't be too difficult to do, should it?

Don't listen to all the Hype, Propaganda and Bullshit – Especially from Oneself!

The web of our life is of a mingled yarn,
good and ill together; our virtues would be proud
if our faults whipped them not; and our crimes
would despair if they were not
cherished by our virtues.

Shakespeare

All propaganda has to be popular
and has to accommodate
itself to the comprehension of the least intelligent
of those whom it seeks to reach.

Adolf Hitler

A large part of waking up to the truth means realising that all is not what it seems. This is primarily for two reasons. The first is that things are dressed up in such a way as to appear different to what they really are. For example, look on a packet of cornflakes the next time you buy them and see if you can find any evidence of corn within the ingredients. In fact they are mostly made out of maize. However, when they were first being marketed it was felt that maize flakes didn't sound as nice and friendly as corn flakes, and so the name *Cornflakes* was born.

In the UK, next time you go to the fish and chip shop, instead of asking for Rock (a fish) and chips ask instead for Dogfish and chips. For that is what Rock really is – Dogfish. But again, it has been felt that the name Dogfish is not very marketable and so it has been changed.

So the naming of things is one way in which propaganda is used to persuade people to think in a particular way about an object, place, or even person. Could anyone ever imagine Marion Morrison being the toughest cowboy of all time? Well, Marion Morrison was, in fact, John Wayne's real name, and it doesn't quite carry the image of his Hollywood persona, does it? Likewise Windscale didn't sound like a very fitting name for a place that had a nuclear power station and so its name was changed to Sellafield. Although when it's finished with, who will be able to sell a field at Sellafield?

The next level of propaganda comes where things are not quite what they seem. Pick up that packet of cornflakes again and look at the ingredients within the packet. There is quite a mind-boggling array of different ingredients, and with so many chemicals in it the average layman would simply have to hope and trust that the scientists putting the ingredients in know what they are doing – but do they?

Products like to advertise themselves as being pure and simple yet often they have artificial processes and flavours within them in order to make them appear to be what the manufacturers want them to be. Artificial colouring, artificial flavouring, artificial preservative, added salt, sugar and water, and goodness knows before long there is very little of the original product left! But the main thing is that it looks great on the shelves! This, plus the packaging and the advertising about the product, can sell it far better in most cases than the integrity and merit of the product itself.

This is something that most people know about but choose to ignore, because to think about it is too much trouble and such matters should be left to the government and health watchdogs to regulate as they know what they are doing. This is a dangerous view to adopt, for governments and such bodies are subject to lobbying from all sorts of groups with vested interests in seeing their products used within other products. Such industries are worth many billions of pounds and the companies involved are not going to give up their profits without a fight.

But more worrying than this is the fact that people are encouraged to package themselves up in certain ways to look better, feel better, smell better with all sorts of alluring promises. These approaches all rely on the fact that the person is in some way not happy with their image or self esteem, and therefore this or that wonder product will help them be and get what they want.

They use gimmicks such as: 'results guaranteed within 28 days or your money back,' or 'new improved formula with some fancy new wonder ingredient with a new mystery product with a fancy scientific sounding name added,' or 'this product will definitely make you more attractive to the opposite sex,' and so on.

At one level most people realise that these claims are probably not true or, at least, exaggerated. However, more powerful than that is the fact that they *want* it to be true and therefore are prepared to suspend their disbelief and give it a try. This says that most people aren't passive victims of propaganda, lies, hype and bullshit, but rather they are willing participants in creating this reality and buy into it willingly.

Hope is a fertile soil into which many seeds can be sown. Once these seeds have been sown all that is needed is the right ingredients for the 'product' to be able to grow.

The prime reason why this works is that people mostly believe that solutions to their problems lie from outside to inside, rather than the other way around. This is how people are conditioned to think and it creates a dependency relationship between the person and their external world. It also makes them vulnerable to inflated promises and hyperbole because, as stated earlier, they want it to be true; they want to believe in it.

A further reason why this strategy succeeds is that people are mostly governed by their ego, which manifests as either a superiority or inferiority complex. Most people have an inferiority complex as the predominant government in their psychology, which explains why they are easily led. Further, society as it is currently configured cannot function with too many leaders, and so the self appointed leaders of fashion, religion, government and opinion decide what views people should have and then set about influencing people to have them.

In truth, however, a superiority and inferiority complex are simply two sides of the same coin, for both are based in a person's insecurity as to who and what they really are. Because of this insecurity they develop a coping behavioural psychology that adopts either a superior or inferior role in their relationships with others. Both are based on external rather than internal criteria, and therefore both are equally brittle when tested. However, they also believe that these external assistances can bolster their esteem and confidence and so they come to rely on them for support. Sometimes they will do this even if there are negative and dangerous side effects involved.

The key weakness that opens the person up to this whole process of autosuggestion is one of abdication of responsibility. For if a person allows others to decide what they should think and why and how, then they can hardly complain if they end up drifting with the tide of conformity where the sea of life is concerned. This is not easy to resist because a person is constantly bombarded from every side with countless conscious and subliminal messages about what they need and why.

In reality people need very little to survive, and in fact live well. However, this doesn't help sell products that don't form part of the basic needs of a person's life. Hence the need for hype, propaganda and bullshit. For who is going to want to buy something unless it is either the best, or the best value for money, or that it guarantees to do something that no other competing product can do?

This all sounds bad enough when thinking about buying products that one needs or thinks one needs. But what about extending this principle into selling oneself to others?

This is what people do in trying to impress others. They use propaganda, hype and bullshit to try and make a good impression in order to convey a sense of status and power, impress a potential partner, get a better job, or whatever. And people think that because those are the rules of the game then it is OK to do it because everyone else does it. So rather than being a conscious deceit it often becomes so automatic and engrained that people do not even realise that they are doing it. It is so second nature that it becomes first nature because people even begin to believe it.

Thus people actually end up believing their very own hype, propaganda and bullshit because the consequences of admitting that it isn't true is too much for them to bear. This clearly is the worst kind of nonsense to believe in because it is self-propagated. Coupled with all the nonsense people have to process coming from other sources, it is understandable that they might get tricked or manipulated in ways that may be out of their control.

But to consciously self-deceive clearly invites trouble, for at some point a person is bound to meet who and what they really are rather than what they think they are or what they want other people to think they are.

This problem again stems from a person's misaligned view of themselves, for they clearly are not happy as they are. Accordingly they assume that other people won't be happy with them as they are either and so they seek to change their appearance. However, they do not wish to make any changes at fundamental level and so they seek a makeover to create the impression that they are something bigger and better than they really are.

The irony here is that often the makeover job doesn't actually make the person look any better. It just makes them think that they do, and because many other people are caught in the same trap they might see the changes as being effective also.

However, these changes cannot be long lasting because they are made at surface level, and at this level fashion changes all the time. So before long the so-called life changing makeover becomes unfashionable and is overtaken by the latest gimmick or fad that no doubt costs a lot of money and will itself be a short term fix.

Now this is not saying that a person shouldn't have a nice haircut or buy themselves something nice to wear or lose weight if they need to. These things are valid at the level of providing enhancement and well-being and in creating a good impression. There is clearly no harm in that and sometimes there is often benefit to be had in doing so. But to base one's centre of gravity in such matters, and to become obsessed by them, is a great mistake.

Human beings do not exist in order that they can have a haircut or wear perfume or follow fashion. They clearly exist for a higher purpose and reason that transcends all such temporal issues. The secret to real success is to find the core pursuit within the life that gives the rest of the life context and meaning. If this is done then a person can better give proper placement to the various pressures and demands in their life, and also all the opportunities.

The truth doesn't need hype, bullshit or spin. It is far too amazing and thrilling as it is for that to be the case.

Take your next breath and know it to be true.

Drugs Can Seriously Damage Your Health
– TV and Newspapers that is.

The media is the most powerful entity on earth.
They have the power to make the innocent
guilty and to make the guilty
innocent, and that's power.
Because they control the minds of the masses.

Malcom X

Drugs are a bet with your mind.

Jim Morrison

Drugs come in many sizes and guises in the world today. Some are legal and remedial for all sorts of illnesses and ailments, from malaria to headaches, to retroviral AIDS drugs, and much more. The drugs industry today is worth trillions of dollars to the world economy. If, for some reason, the human race suddenly developed a super immunity level that meant that none of these drugs were required any longer, then the side effect of that would be that the world economy would collapse. This is because there are literally millions of jobs that are tied up in the drugs industry with trillions of dollars invested in it. If that were no longer needed then the stock markets of the world would all collapse, millions of people would suddenly be out of employment and a huge depression would ensue.

Perhaps this is ironic because there are also countless drugs that are used to manage, control or cure depression, but no drug has yet been invented that can cure economic depression! And, just in case you were thinking it, no, money doesn't cure economic depression, although, yes, it is a drug!

As things stand at the moment the human race does still have an apparent need for these so-called remedial drugs and so the drug companies, their shareholders and workers can all breathe a huge sigh of relief. However, just how much these drugs are actually needed is open to debate. For sometimes lifestyle plus the wrong diet and use of other medicines and prescriptions can, in fact, cause a compounding of problems in a person's immune system whereby they become a veritable drug addict. Not the kind that is addicted to banned narcotics, but is addicted to the effects of either relief from pain or a general sense of feeling better than they felt before taking the drug.

Some of these prescribed drugs do address the cause of an illness and therefore are a valuable development in trying to control disease and make people's living standard better. This is especially so in the third world where many of the population are living with diseases that could be easily treated with the right medication. The reason why these diseases aren't treated is usually down to money because the people who have the disease can't afford to pay the prices demanded for the drugs by the drugs companies. The drugs companies, in turn, won't lower the prices because that would reduce their margins and also create a dangerous precedent in that people in the West might demand lower prices to match those being charged in the third world.

Despite the fact that many of these drugs are valuable and useful their use is governed by market forces and the politics of economics. Also some of them do have side effects that are unfortunate and, in some cases, the overuse of such drugs can cause greater long term negative effects than their initial benefits. This has already started to happen with the use of antibiotics, for when they were first discovered they had incredible success in fighting bugs. What wasn't appreciated at the time was that the bugs were themselves able to mutate and, over time, develop immunity to the antibiotics. This then led to the need to develop better and stronger antibiotics, which in turn led to the bugs getting stronger, and so on. The worrying signs at the moment are that the number of antibiotics available to treat illness is dangerously low, and in some cases none of them work any more.

The human race has always had a relationship with what could be called drugs or natural remedies. Tribal cultures all researched and discovered the therapeutic properties of plants and herbs within their environments and have been using them for many thousands of years quite successfully. Many of these remedies have been passed down to us today and are still used by us today either directly, as the ancients used them, or more commonly they have been incorporated into the remedies adopted by the drugs companies. More commonly, however, the drug companies seek to find and use chemical and synthetic substitutes for the natural sources because these are easier and cheaper to make and also the profit margins are greater.

Therefore the use of drugs is both widespread and plentiful with much of it genuinely assisting the quality of life of many people. But the use of drugs is not simple because every drug has a side effect. Also long term use of drugs, both at individual and societal level, causes genetic and constitutional changes that can have negative effects that may greatly outweigh any short term benefits.

Other well-known drugs that are used are things like alcohol, cigarettes, tea and coffee. These are all legal for adults to purchase in most countries, subject to certain bans in some Muslim states, for example. But generally they are available and legal. These are called social drugs, although most people who take them wouldn't like for them to be called drugs because this connotes a sense that there is something wrong with taking them.

Not so long ago these items, especially cigarettes and alcohol, were regarded as being socially acceptable. Whilst advertising still seeks to make them trendy, the position is somewhat moderated today with clear medical evidence showing that even passive smoking can cause serious illnesses.

The position with coffee and tea is much more moderate but they also have addictive properties within them and, with too much consumption, unfortunate side affects can occur. Like cigarettes and alcohol they can have their addictive aspects to them, if usage isn't monitored carefully.

The next level regarding the use of drugs relates to what are often called recreational and hard drugs. This includes things such as marijuana, ecstasy, LSD, heroin, cocaine, amphetamines, opium, and so on. The use of these drugs is prohibited by law in most countries. All of these drugs, to one degree or another, change a person's state of consciousness – for good or for ill – and therefore change their reality. Some say that these changes are mind warping and others say that they are mind altering into higher states.

Whatever the case, most are, to one degree or another, addictive and in the long term are damaging to the person, both physically and mentally. The harder the drugs the worse the distortion of reality, and also the more addictive they are. Anything that is this addictive is not healthy and, because these harder drugs are illegal, the person usually spirals out of control as they somehow need to fund their habit, which is very expensive due to the fact that the drugs themselves are illegal.

Because the drugs are illegal it is therefore a criminal offence to be in possession of them and use them. However, their illegality is, in truth, a much lesser reason for not taking them than the fact of the damage they do to the person in terms of escapism and dependency. These reasons should be sufficient to ward people off taking them but that doesn't appear to be the case and so the government has to make them illegal. This, in its own reverse psychology way, is the very reason why many people are drawn to them in the first place.

Another reason for banning the drugs is because of what a person taking them might do, either under the influence of them or as a side-effect, such as criminal activity in order to get money for them. The latter is a circular argument in many ways because if the drugs were made legal and their production regulated then they wouldn't cost so much on the black market. People who used them would then be less likely to have to rob other people to pay for their habit. This does not advocate that they should be made legal but simply points out the anomaly in trying to deal with the problem.

It also serves to point out that people who do use such strong drugs become dependent upon them, and therefore because of this fact the behaviour becomes erratic and unpredictable.

This point should not be lost on the next category of class A drugs – the media. In particular this is referring to TV and newspapers. For both these elements of the media display classic symptoms of what may be termed drug culture in that they are both addictive and also mind altering in a dangerous way if not controlled.

This is not saying that all media is evil and should be avoided, for sometimes it can be most informative and useful. Like all the other forms of drugs their use should be regulated and monitored, and in some cases banned altogether. The first place of censorship shouldn't be the government but a person's own filter systems as to what is useful and what isn't.

Most of the world's media today is in the control of a very few people and they often have their own agenda and profile that they wish to serve up to the public. It is generally assumed that the public decides what they will watch, and thereby determine the scheduling and content of programmes, but this is not the case. For if people are fed something often enough, and for long enough, they will eventually get to like it – whether they like it or not!

This is especially so today with the incredible proliferation of the digital and internet age whereby a person can access countless TV channels and even more internet sites, which all pedal their own version of truth.

An important point to look at in respect of the truth is the news media in its various forms. A person looks at the newspaper or watches the news on TV to find out what is happening in the world. Or so they think. But all these media are subject to editorial processes in that someone has to decide what is and isn't important, how it should be reported, and with what angle or bias. Then there is also the angle or spin of those who are making the news to consider. For people want their position to be presented in a particular light and so will couch their position accordingly. This is known as spin.

All this is known and mostly understood, but yet it still manages to get past most people's radar and is assimilated into their opinion factory where their opinions are formed. Opinions need data upon which they can form up, and there is plenty of it out there.

The other side of this news media process is what doesn't get reported. For lack of coverage is just as telling as what is reported. In fact, it is often more so because usually someone somewhere wants the information suppressed and/or kept out of the public domain. Governments do this all the time by consciously withholding information, editing its release selectively, and seeking to downplay its significance wherever possible. As a British diplomat responded a few years ago when he was accused of lying in relation to an espionage case, he stated that he wasn't lying but rather was being economical with the truth.

Governments also try and time their releases of bad news carefully so that it gets buried amongst other 'more important' news and therefore relegated to the minor items of that day or even ignored completely.

All this contributes to what many people regard as being the dumbing down of the media and its processes. This is particularly so today because we live in the age of the sound bite. Because people's attention spans are so poor, media representatives know that unless they move on to the next item quickly they will lose people's attention, and if that is the case then they might tune in to a rival. This is why on radio and TV the presenters often say to guests that they would love to spend more time opening up the subject in question, but they need to move on to the next item. This is simply not true. They do have time to further it but they choose not to for the reasons previously stated.

All this is made worse by the quality, or lack of it, in the media itself. This dumbing down applies at all levels from news, to gossip columns, to soap operas, and so on. And the worse it gets the more people become addicted to it, and somehow they start to integrate their own reality with that of what they read, see or hear. They may not think that this is the case, but the power of the media to influence and change how and what people think is huge.

This is because most people do not have the ability to activate their own discernment gene. Rather they just adopt views and opinions from the menu of opinions that they are served up by others. Whilst in some cases there may be a choice of opinions available on the menu, in other cases there isn't. Whatever the case, the person certainly has limited choice as to what they can pick and choose to believe, and usually they are quite happy to believe what they are told because that saves them the work of having to do it for themselves.

After all, the news is meant to be impartial, isn't it? Yet the angle at which any particular event is looked at changes the perception of what has actually occurred. This is why politicians do interviews in order that they can place an emphasis on the facts to support the version of reality that they want the voters to believe. In this there are the two great arts of propaganda: what you say and what you don't say. For an over or under emphasis changes and often distorts the real facts of the matter.

This is then further reinforced by the next great rule of propaganda, which is that if you say something often enough then people will eventually start to believe it. At first people may be sceptical about the view being expressed, but after a while it starts to get into their subconscious mind and slowly their resistance to the view can be worn away until they either agree or simply don't care any more. This technique is further enhanced by the offering of subtle variations on the view being expressed so that it seems to be true from more than one angle.

Also there is the technique of offering what is called hard and soft positions. The hard position is the one that people most want to hear, but this is usually caveated with a softer position that leaves the door open for this position to later replace the hard position. For example, a government may say that it is not going to develop any more nuclear power stations (hard position) unless and until all other reasonable alternative sources of energy have been explored and found to be less viable in the circumstances (soft position). By stating the soft option as a tag-on alternative, the door is then easily opened for the government to find the research it needs to 'prove' that the nuclear option is the only viable option to adopt to solve the energy crisis.

They can then easily justify their position by saying that they did an extensive review of it, whilst in fact having already made up their mind in advance of any research being done. They simply use this tactic as a means of sowing the idea in the public's mind and then later firming that position up with the 'evidence' to support the argument that they really wish to put forward.

This situation is further compounded by the so-called democratic systems of government in the world. In this system, the elected government puts forward a policy that it wishes to adopt and the opposition opposes it. The reason for this is not necessarily to put forward a better policy, but rather to make the elected government look bad and weak so that people would rather vote for the opposition next time. Therefore the real reason for this so-called democratic process is the seeking after power rather than looking for the best solution to the problems and issues facing the country.

If all parties did look at the truth of the issue in the bigger picture, then they would surely try to agree a best way forward together rather than simply opposing each other for the sake of it.

An example of this is in the energy field itself where if all parties stopped and paused and looked at the true reality they would accept that, unless radical changes are made to the supply and use of energy, things will get much worse in the future before they get better. This is because of the West's dependency on oil and fossil fuels for energy.

As this is being written Britain is deciding its future where energy use is concerned, and the political consensus is swinging towards returning to using nuclear energy. The persuasive argument being put forward to justify this move is that nuclear energy is 'clean' in that it produces no carbon dioxide emissions. Therefore this will enable Britain to meet its obligations where lowering of CO_2 emissions is concerned. This argument sounds attractive to some but, of course, it is a deceit upon the truth.

For not only does nuclear power leave a much greater polluting footprint than any other form of energy, in that the waste by-products take thousands of years to clean up, but also producing such energy does pollute of its own account. In this regard nuclear reactors need Uranium in order to produce nuclear power and Uranium is quite a rare substance, certainly in its purest form. If, therefore, numerous more nuclear reactors were built to fuel the need for energy, then this would mean a massive increase in demand for Uranium. This in turn would mean that the supplies of Uranium would dwindle very quickly, to such a degree that supplies of premium grade Uranium would be depleted within ten years.

There would be lesser grade Uranium stores left but these are less pure and would involve sophisticated extraction techniques, which are themselves polluting in nature. In fact the pollution caused by the extraction of such lesser grade Uranium would outweigh the benefits gained by using so-called clean nuclear power.

The real reason the governments shy away from offering real solutions to real problems is twofold:

1. Because they are heavily lobbied by the energy companies, who have huge weight and clout in the decision making process.
2. The political cost of taking such tough but necessary decisions would, in their view, be catastrophic and so they avoid making such decisions.

The truth is that in the long term renewable sources of energy of energy are cheaper, cleaner and more sustainable. There is no doubt about that fact whatsoever. However, to accept that fact requires a change of mindset and behaviour for all concerned. And this change is one from a being a consumer to being a responsible player in the greater dynamics of inter-relationship and inter-support between the Earth and the human race.

These issues transcend politics to a massive degree, but politicians won't let them. That is until the point of reckoning when they can no longer put their finger of power in the dyke of the future onsetting.

In this the media is somewhat conspiratorial in this process. For mostly they represent what the politicians want to have represented, and this then usually ends up being a debate between diametrically opposed views, neither of which represents a constructive way forward, for both parties know that to champion the greater truth would constitute political suicide. So all parties engage in the greatest conspiracy theory of them all, and that is the suppression of the truth by a process of misinformation and disinformation in the hope that a badly informed public will make badly informed decisions and accept the so-called solutions offered by their leaders.

Politics and the media are about style rather than substance – and they flatter to deceive.

Therefore the only way for a person to find the truth is to wean themselves off these drugs and begin to think and act for themselves.

Who knows, they may even vote for themselves rather than someone else to represent them. Whether or not they do depends on how much they are prepared to trust themselves.

The Matter with or the Matter of Relationships

If civilization is to survive, we
must cultivate the science
of human relationships – the ability
of all peoples, of all kinds,
to live together, in the same world at peace.

Franklin D. Roosevelt

Almost all of our relationships
begin and most of them
continue as forms of mutual exploitation,
a mental or physical barter, to be terminated when
one or both parties run out of goods.

W. H. Auden

The main key to successful living lies in making relationships work. This is important because, as John Donne famously said, "No man is an island."

We are all part of the mainland, to one degree or another, and therefore we need to find the ways to make our relationships work. Because if they do then they are more beneficial and rewarding. If they don't work then they become stressful and antagonistic, and this in turn leads to conflict.

The title of this chapter focuses on the word *matter*, and this is done deliberately because of the associated meanings of the word. For matter in this context can mean both what is wrong with relationships and the actual physical content of relationships. It is proposed to explore the concept of relationships further with this aspect.

In physical sciences there are three states of matter that are generally regarded as existing: solid, liquid and gas. Generally a substance is regarded as being in one state or the other at any given time, although this state can change from one to another according to circumstances. For example, water, steam and ice are three states of the same thing that are governed by temperature; the higher temperatures causing it to gravitate more towards water and steam and the lower temperatures causing it to move towards water and ice.

Whilst there may be points of cross-over – where more than one of these states is at play at the same time where the individual molecules change their binding relationships with other molecules and thereby their states from, say, liquid to gas – nevertheless a substance is generally regarded as being either in one state or another.

But what if it were possible for all three states to co-exist at the same time so that it was possible for the substance in question to be solid, liquid and gas all at once? For water has the potential to be ice, water and steam all at the same time. Which one it becomes depends on which temperature is applied to it. But what if more than one temperature could be applied to it, or at least different parts of it, at the same time?

This suggests that it might be possible for what could be called a plasma state to be applied to relationships; to make them have elements of solid, liquid or gas applied to them all at the same time to help them work better. What is meant by plasma in this context is a highly charged and conductive state that is full of possibilities.

The point being made here is that relationships tend to become fixed and narrower over time, and therefore more matter based. This is where things start to matter in the wrong way.

Relationships need to have elements of solid, liquid and gas for them to work effectively and successfully, because if they become locked in just one or the other they can develop problems.

If they are just gaseous then they become volatile and anything can happen. They can spontaneously combust into anything from high euphoria and excitement to highly dangerous explosions that can hurt people. The point about such relationships is that they aren't stable.

Relationships that are fluid are just that. On the positive side they can be flexible and adaptable but on the negative side they can be lukewarm and wishy-washy. They have no real high points and no real low points either. They tend, therefore, to drift along on the sea of life and let things take them where the tide of life is going.

If relationships are purely solid then the up side is that they are firm, reliable and guaranteed. The down side is that they become inflexible and based in dogma and unable to change.

All relationships are based on these principles and some become more based in one aspect than the others. The key to success is maintaining the plasma state where all three natures co-exist at the same time. The more fixed a relationship becomes the more physical it is. What is meant by this is that it becomes more and more known and fixed in its nature. This can apply to any of the above states, for some relationships become fixed in being volatile and some become fixed in always doing the same things in the same way.

Generally what happens when people get into fixed relationships is that they start to use each other for their own particular needs or requirements. The problem with this is that the more a person uses other people the less they use of themselves. The more this happens the more the state of plasma lessens, or the less spark there is in the relationship.

This can be seen quite easily in terms of what might be called the 'falling in love' relationship. When a couple first meet and start falling in love then everything is highly charged and plasmagenic. If anything the balance is much more towards the gaseous end of the state of matter and a high state of flux exists between the couple. This creates an opportunity for a flow of electricity between them. In this state nothing is the matter.

However, as the relationship progresses so does its state, for if this initial falling in love stage is survived (and often it doesn't because being in love is highly volatile) then the couple move on to the next stage, which is starting to think about the future together. If they decide that they want to spend their future together they start to think about 'settling down' and this is where things start to become more solid.

This of itself is not a good or a bad thing. It simply might be a natural progression in the relationship, and this is fine providing it is not a substitute for the spark no longer being there. So there is nothing else to do except what everyone else does, which is to get married. If that is all that the relationship develops into then it becomes too solid and stuck and will cause problems later when people start to wonder why they have ended up in the position they have and then question where the magic has gone.

The key to successful relationships is having a balance of all three states at play all the time as this prevents the relationship becoming fixed and keeps it fresh and evolving for both parties. In this way the parties keep discovering new and interesting things about themselves and each other.

Indeed this applies to all relationships and not just to couples. It can be seen in how nations, states, religions and ideologies view and deal with each other. The exact same principles apply, for if the relationships do not keep the three states at play then the parties tend to become fixed in their views about themselves and each other. The more this happens the more they become fundamentalist in their views and less tolerant of the other party.

This is usually because one or both of the parties becomes too fixed in their own views about what is right and wrong, and as they become more entrenched in those views they tend to project them on to the other party. The irony is that they tend to accuse the other of being extremist and fundamentalist whilst they themselves are tarred with the same brush, perhaps just painted a different colour.

The way that relationships can work and develop over time is that they keep moving forward about things that both parties regard as being important and that are shared values. When relationships go wrong it is usually because they cannot find any common ground and this is mostly because the relationship has become one of personal rather than shared interest. When interests are personal there can only be conflict because everyone is different and their personal needs also differ.

However, if the relationship is based on building something together, and that stays at the core or heart of the relationship, then the parties are much better placed to work things out, compromise and adapt to each other's needs. Inside a mutual interest and shared purpose there is always going to be plenty of give and take – and not just taking!

The word *relating* anagrams to *integral*, and the best way of continuing to develop a relationship is to regularly keep coming back to what is important about it. This process also helps to relegate the small and petty differences that are always going to occur because it will keep them in context. It is when these differences are not kept in context that they can get blown out of all proportion and develop into full blown crises and even war.

The search for the integral will, if pursued, cause the parties to find something deeper and richer in the relationship. It will cause them to see what they share and not what they are missing. This is very important today for people are often confronted in life with what they lack and not what they already have. In other words, they are educated to see that the glass is half empty rather than half full.

The truth is that the glass, in most people's lives, is overflowing with blessings.

The other aspect in this *relating/integral* relationship is that these two words also anagram to *altering*. This suggests that if the parties in the relationship are relating about what is integral and really important then change is inevitable.

This is often seen as a bad or difficult thing in relationships because one or both of the parties is threatened by the other party changing. This speaks again of a relationship having become fixed in the wrong way and based in possession or requirement.

Change based around growth and refinement is the healthiest thing in the world. To seek to impose change, or to prevent it in another, is a tyranny, but to allow and encourage it in another is a great service.

As Ghandi said, "Be the change that you want to see in the world." But at the same time let others, especially those you love and care about, be the change that they want to see in the world too. In doing so, you let them help you be the change that you wish to be.

Language

A word is dead when it is said, some say.
I say it just begins to live that day.

Emily Dickinson

Words are also actions, and
actions are a kind of words.

Ralph Waldo Emerson

Any consideration of the esoteric nature of human beings has to begin with language. For language, in its many forms, constitutes an amazing means of communication at very many levels.

Language is very esoteric and marks a huge octave leap between human beings and all other life forms on the planet. Within language are the most amazing, profound and hidden codings and understandings to enable better appreciation of the human condition. And whilst it is appreciated that animals communicate in much more sophisticated ways than previously thought, clearly human language contains far greater complexities and subtleties. Accordingly the gap between human and animal levels of communication is simply staggering.

Yet what is the nature of language unto itself?

At a simple level it is a means of communication and conveyance of information, understanding, meaning, and essence and frequency transference. Wow! If that is the simple level, what is the complicated one?

There are two primary types of language being examined here – spoken and written. Almost all cultures in the world have evolved both kinds in some shape or form. There are, of course, other forms of indirect language, such as body language, art, music, religious practices, ceremonies, and so on that convey something from the culture and what it represents. For our current purposes, however, the two main forms of language – spoken and written – will be researched.

In order for language to convey anything at all its meaning has to be understood. For example, until the Rosetta Stone was discovered the written language of ancient Egypt could not be understood. Once the code within the Rosetta Stone was revealed the whole meaning of the ancient Egyptian texts could be appreciated.

This same principle applies equally to the spoken aspects of all languages. For unless a person understands the grammar and syntax of Swahili when it is spoken to them, there will be little or no meaning to the sounds that they hear and it will remain a complete mystery them.

The first level of unlocking the esoteric meaning of language begins with the literal meaning of words and sentences and what they contain. However, there are many more subtle levels to language, and this has been appreciated for as long as language has existed.

Even at a very simple level, think how esoteric it actually is to be able to read this book. Consider the fact that, in reality, all a person is doing is looking at black marks on a page of white paper. Yet people are able to obtain meaning from it and, not only that, but feelings and sensations as well. This is clearly a huge development from the flora and fauna worlds where the messages have to be more rudimentary and basic.

Effective writing can convey images, impressions, sensations and feelings and activate the senses in exactly the same way as the more carnal messages of the flora and fauna worlds do. It is simply a more sophisticated and developed means of doing so.

Within this there are two further aspects to consider. One of these is the actual message locked up and held within language itself, and the other is the ability to interpret them by those who receive the messages.

Within the evolution of language, from the level of cave man *'ug!'* to the incredible variety and virtuosity of language today, there has clearly been a whole journey of refinement. People like Shakespeare knew this very well indeed for he created a vast number of new words for the English language.

It has been claimed that approximately one in ten words in his plays were brand new ones that he himself created, not to mention many of the phrases and sayings that we still use today. This is quite an extraordinary amount of creativity and speaks of an ability to not only understand the human condition, but also to be able to find ways of conveying that to others.

He did this because there were new feelings, emotions, natures and frequencies that he wished to capture and express, and so old words would not adequately describe the senses he was trying to convey. This not only relates to individual words but also through such things as turn of phrase, nuance, sayings, maxims, sentiments, morals, timing, rhythm, and much more.

In terms of rhythm alone consider, for example, Iambic Pentameter, which was often used in writing sonnets. The double beat (or 'iamb') almost mirrors the rhythm of the heart and has a definite pulsating affect that causes much more than a simple registration in the brain of the literal meaning of the words.

Thus language, or at least its potential, has become incredibly sophisticated and diverse in its capabilities and possibilities as a working tool for communication of all sorts of natures, emotions, feelings and frequencies.

Also every person has a totally unique way of expressing themselves. No two people have the same voice, speak in the same way, use the same emphasis, have the same exact accent, and so on.

A baby, when responding to its mother's voice, does not actually 'understand' the words being spoken but responds to the rhythms and frequencies within the mother's voice. The converse is also true, for the mother can often recognise her baby's cry amongst a group of other babies because the child's cry is as unique as its thumbprint or smell.

It is also known that rhythms and frequencies in a person's speech can reveal whether or not they are telling the truth, and machines such as lie detectors can now measure the subtle differences. By deduction this says that people too can detect these differences, no matter how subtle they might be.

By analogy, it is well known that the human sense of smell is much greater than is generally accepted. This is because people in the West no longer really have a need for it. Yet think how acute a wine taster's sense of smell is, or that of a Kalahari bushman when detecting the different smells of animals.

Consider also the whole feature of accents and dialects. These are fascinating for they seem to evolve their own character and style according to a host of different factors. This happens to such a degree that where a person comes from can be determined to within five miles simply because of their accent. Why does it work in this way? Could it be that language is influenced by the land in which it arises? It is curious that there are so many different languages and accents with such diversity in frequency, nature, rhythm, tone, pitch, and vibration.

Language must therefore be truly esoteric at core, for why else would the word 'spelling' be used when it comes to writing down words and their meaning? Could it mean that words actually cast a spell? Certainly, if written by or spoken by the right person they would seem to do so. Think of the writings of Shakespeare, Dickens and the Bronte sisters; or the power of the speeches by people such as Churchill, Martin Luther King and John F Kennedy. They knew of the power and influence of language and its ability to shape people and to be shaped by them.

Language at core is entirely esoteric, but the degree of its esoteric influence depends upon the breadth and scope of its usage. Shakespeare, for example, is said to have had a working vocabulary of 30–40,000 words. Recent studies have shown that most people today only have a working vocabulary of 1,500–2,000 words, although many use even less than 1,000 words regularly. With this being the case most usage is for, what could be termed, trading language rather than its more core esoteric aspects.

The platform out from which language is used determines how causative and potent it is. It is like using different ingredients in cooking. The more variety of foods, herbs and spices that are available the more options there are to create different combinations of foods.

It is good to broaden one's usage and knowledge of language, for it is like a tool waiting to be used to optimum effect.

So here are some technologies for broadening one's talents where language is concerned.

Firstly, try and learn a new word every day for a month. Flick through the dictionary until you find a word you are not familiar with that has some force or significance for you or that simply catches your attention. Then try and use that word as often as possible during the day in a conscious and deliberate way. See what that causes and then try and discover the nature of the word unto itself. See how it relates to other words and how it works in different contexts.

Secondly, think about a word you already know and wish to research at a deeper level; say something like hope, care, value, love, humanity, try, will, inspiration, etc. Use a creative and positive word. Again, do this for a month using a different word every day and as often as you can during the day. Assess and detect its influence and effect. Try and sense its deeper meaning and connections and how and when it would be used to greatest effect, for mostly words are used in a general and diluted way, making them less powerful or, at least, less esoteric than normal.

In doing these exercises it is possible to find that not only does it broaden and improve a person's range of language and vocabulary, but it will also deepen a persons' value for language, causing them to want to use it more effectively and purposefully.

Language is a self-instruction and self-printing process every time it is used, whether written, spoken or thought. Like any powerful tool it should be used carefully, for what can cure can also inflict. It is important to remember its power and potency for self-diagnosis and coding because if a person tells themselves something often enough it becomes printed at a deeper level and then affects the behaviour and response systems.

Accordingly it is not wise for a person to tell themselves that they are a failure at anything, for that is a dangerous thing to do because they are printing their systems with failure. Perhaps that is why it is said that there are two types of written language: writing (righting?) and printing?

It is wise, therefore, to use language in as constructive a sense as possible towards what a person is trying to build in their life. People construct sentences with words in much the same way as they build a house, so it is important to put the right bricks in the right place. To do otherwise will lead to it falling down.

Is it mere co-incidence that in the Bible it says: "In the beginning was the Word?" This must be a very powerful concept, for the first thing that God supposedly did was to speak, and the first thing that God said was, "Let there be light." And there was. This was quite a statement to begin the Creation process!

If the first thing that was created was light, this suggests that the first place to think about using language from is to spread more light into the world. If that is what the Creation did then surely it would be wise for humans to follow suit.

It is suggested that the polarity of language, and how it is used, is vital. Often people are trained to use language from the standpoint of looking at what is wrong and how to make that better. Yet truly the human situation is one of there being so much that is already right. Therefore the challenge is to seek to make things even better. After all, there seems to be far more things working in the human race's favour than against it, so that has to be a good platform out from which to proceed.

Finally, as a point of notation, within this book the reader will often note that things like anagrams are used to try and illustrate particular points that are being made. Classic education would try to dismiss this process as merely a co-incidence or some kind of gimmick. But is it? Anagrams and hidden meanings within language have been used for as long as language itself has been in use. Ancient people knew that there were ways to insert deeper meanings within a text to convey another level of understanding to those who have the eyes to see or the ears to hear.

To get a different meaning all that is needed is to rearrange the ingredients (letters) into a different combination. Perhaps this esoteric art doesn't just apply to Language?

This poses the question: what might *you* be an anagram of, and what could you anagram to?

The Most Important Word Ever

A word after a word after a word is power.
Margaret Atwood

All the great things are simple, and many can be
expressed in a single word:
freedom, justice, honour, duty, mercy, hope.
Winston Churchill

This section suggests that there is one word in the English language that is more important than any other.

The reader is invited to come up with their own word first and then turn the page to see the word that has been chosen.

The word is:

WHY?

And why why?

The most causative of processes for human beings is their ability to question and reason things through. It is the burning desire to know, to find out, to discover, to sense, to feel that propels human beings forward in their search for truth

The word 'why' is the key to every door where knowledge and wisdom are concerned. It is every child's favourite question. People have no doubt experienced the situation where a child has asked a question to which an answer is given. As a result of which the question 'Why?' appears again and again. This either drives the adult into their own awe and wonder and questioning process or, perhaps more commonly, into a 'because I say so' response.

This 'Why?' approach to learning is often driven out of people at a very young age as children are educated towards conformity-like behaviour patterns with set 'answers' to learn and syllabuses to follow. In reality most modern education takes people away from what they really are and turns them into what they are not, e.g. doctor, lawyer, teacher, nurse, rather than trying to develop what they already are. This may seem like a minor distinction but the truth is that there is a massive divergence between the two approaches. These differences highlight, and call into sharp relief, some of the problems that modern education faces when trying to equip children for the future.

Questioning the 'system' of education could undermine the very structure on which it is based, and so conformity is demanded if a person wishes to succeed on the journey of becoming what they have not yet become. This means that the vast majority of people become sheep-like in their behaviour and dulled down from the experience of life at its most wondrous.

The author remembers holding his just turned two year old niece outside on a summer's evening as it was changing from dusk to evening and she being filled with the wonder and awe of the change from light to dark. She simply looked up at the sky and said, "Getting dark." She did not really know what that meant but was totally captivated by what was happening.

When he was asked why it was getting dark the author replied, "Sun gone to bed," and in her searching for feeling and meaning she kept whispering the words, "Sun gone to bed," and each time another star appeared, as it got progressively darker, she would look up and say, "New Star". In that moment there was the sense for the author that he was the student and the niece was the teacher.

Her total openness and wonder and awe caused the garden and everything in it and the sky above to come alive and be made magic by the experience. Couple this with the fact that shortly thereafter her five year old sister came in with the mind boggling question: "Is the sky alive?"

The word 'Why?' is therefore a marvellous starter into anything at all because it does one thing brilliantly well, which is to activate the search to find out the reasons for things.

The trail of 'why', if followed carefully and diligently, will lead a person to the core reasons as to why humans are alive and how what they do can make a difference.

And why is that important? What a good question!

Indifference

*At the bottom of enmity between
strangers lies indifference.*

Soren Kierkegaard

*To correct a natural indifference
I was placed half-way
between misery and the Sun. Misery kept me from
believing that all was well under the Sun,
and the Sun taught me that
history wasn't everything.*

Albert Camus

This is possibly the worst disease that human beings can suffer from. For it speaks of not caring. The gesture that belongs with this state is a shrug of the shoulders and a 'so what, what does it matter?' attitude. This behaviour has significantly contributed to the state of human disconnection and also perpetuates its reality.

It abdicates from, and relinquishes responsibility to, everything outside and often inside oneself.

One aspect of understanding indifference is illustrated by seeing it as two words:

IN DIFFERENCE

The greater the level of indifference, the greater the distance between the person and the unity that exists within is. The real power in things lies in unity and not within the cultural concept of divide and rule. Ultimately that can only ever be self-defeating as the thing that divides must, in time, be divided itself.

It is often said that opposites attract, and an example of this is the positive and negative ends of a magnet attracting each other. However, at an esoteric level it is sameness that attracts in that each part attracts the missing and higher bit of itself from the other, and in each other they find union not difference.

It was when humans began to see themselves as different and superior to other life forms on Earth that serious problems began.

The choice is simple in how humans need to address the issues they face.

Humans need to *unite* in order that they can *untie* the horrible mess that they have got themselves into.

The thing that will *unite* people is the premise around which they choose to be the same.

This is the promise of what it means to be responsible, living on a sacred, beautiful, living planet. And human beings have an integrating and not disintegrating part to play within the Earth's balances and processes. In truth, nobody owns anything because all belongs to all, for all is part of all. This is an important and fundamental understanding that humans need to embrace.

We are not indifferent to the fact of needing to breathe the air, and yet we seem largely to be indifferent to what things we fill the air with. There is a subpoena upon us to fill our lungs with air in order that we may live. However, there is also a subpoena upon us all to live in order that we may breathe.

Apathy and indifference undermine the very marrow of our existence. We share this experience called 'living' for such a short time on this tiny blue marble that floats magically through space and time. Can we but pause and feel the beauty and majesty of our gift and together be moved?

And if we are moved then indifference is banished from our species forever.

Intelligence

*You cannot teach a man anything; you can only
help him find it within himself.*

Galileo Gallilei

*I've always felt that a person's intelligence is
directly reflected by the number of
conflicting points of view
they can entertain simultaneously
on the same topic.*

Abigail Adams

This is a crucial yet elusive subject to research in understanding the human condition, for it is key to any decision making process. Yet, what actually is intelligence beyond book or factual information?

As a test, try the following exercise. People think they know what intelligence is for they assume they understand what another person means when they use that word. Or at least they think they do.

Before turning the page write down what your definition of intelligence is.

Having done that, turn the page and read on.

Now look again at your definition of intelligence.

Is it primarily related to some kind of brain cleverness? Most western people's definition of intelligence is. Is it more scientific or technical in its nature, and does it refer to having been educated or schooled in some way? Again, most western perception of intelligence is brain orientated, and the reason for that is quite simply that most western education is to do with training the brain. It is hardly surprising that the brain describes what *it* does as being the definition of intelligence!

Being able to do very long quadratic equations doesn't necessarily make a person intelligent. It is simply an ability to do long quadratic equations. On its own it is useless, for it sits like a fish out of water.

Intelligence, therefore, is relative and depends upon context.

Consider who is more intelligent – a nuclear scientist or an aborigine tribe elder? When it comes to their specialist subjects the nuclear scientist is more intelligent about designing nuclear reactors and the aborigine is more intelligent when considering how to live and survive in the outback of Australia.

Consider whether literacy is a sign of intelligence. Most people would say yes, but again that comes out from a western mindset and western context. Nomadic tribes of the world may not be able to read black ink on paper but they can read the seasons, know how to find water and food when they need it, and can read the wind.

There is in the West a value judgement that its kind of intelligence is best. This does not mean that all Western 'intelligence' is bad. It clearly isn't. What it simply goes to show is that all so-called intelligence is derived out of experience and the context of its environment.

Being able to read a map of the London Underground is very useful to Londoners, but it is of no use to an Inuit Indian who is trying to find ways to catch seals and fish. The reverse applies in equal measure in that knowing how to catch fish and seals won't get you round the London Underground system!

At local level the first thing that can be said about intelligence is that there are no absolutes, only different degrees of ability. Some tribal people have different skills at catching fish, and therefore are more intelligent where that activity is concerned, whilst others may be skilled at finding water.

In the West some market analysts are better than others and therefore do better. Knowing how to catch seals is not going to help analyse what the stock market is doing.

Therefore at this level intelligence is local and governed by local circumstance and need.

Consider how intelligent the first human that was able to control fire must have seemed to his tribe or culture. They would probably have been given demigod or sacred magician status at the time but he or she probably wouldn't score very highly on an Intelligence Quotient (IQ) test. Yet most people with an IQ over 150 do not know how to start a fire in the wild without a box of matches.

Another inroad into the research of intelligence lies in the fact that as humans evolve their 'intelligence' changes according to their local circumstance. Yet, even as this evolving process occurs, some kinds of intelligence get lost and others get born. For example, as humans evolved and migrated to different parts of the Earth some kinds of local intelligence were lost on the journey and others acquired. This is why there are not many Saharan desert nomads that know how to fish, nor are there any plains Indians in America who know how to train and handle elephants.

This also applies to things such as diet and medicine, for before modern mass mobility at artificial speeds humans could only use what was around them to supply all their needs for living. In this regard much knowledge was gathered in respect of such needs and passed down from generation to generation in a 'catching the way of it' method rather than by formal, textbook learning. This process is also common in the animal kingdom where learned responses are passed on from the older animals to younger ones.

It is therefore worth considering, at this point, whether animals, and even plants, are in any way intelligent? This depends on what the workable definition of intelligence may be. More consideration will be given to that point later in this chapter.

Perhaps this first level of intelligence, which is mainly to do with the physical worlds and the environment that living things find themselves in, could be called:

Primary / Design Intelligence

All living creatures have this in some shape or form, otherwise they could not survive, grow and flourish, and secure the continuance of their species. Within this is a natural context for the species whereby they become an integrated part of the whole ecology within which they live. They are therefore subject to regulation and control by that ecology, rather than being able to manage or control it to any large degree. Species that struggle to survive within the ecology offered by their local circumstance have three choices:

1. Adapt
2. Migrate to a different ecology where their particular features can safely exist
3. Become extinct

Of the three choices the third definitely looks like being the least intelligent, although it is estimated that more than 99% of all species that previously existed on Earth are now extinct. Human beings are now facing the real possibility of extinction themselves unless they find the right kind of intelligence to help them change their ways and be more responsible in the affairs of Nature and the Planet.

Within this aspect of primary intelligence no one system is dominant in the ecosystem itself for it is all integrated and inter-connected. The design of each species has evolved over countless millions of years to its current form, which enables it to become integrated within its environment.

It is often said that it is only the strong that survive. This is not actually true, for it is only the more highly evolved that survive.

Primary intelligence, therefore, is common to all living things, for their working parts and adaptation skills are such that they are able to survive and continue to function as a part of their local and planetary ecology. Organisms develop this intelligence in order to relate to their own systems and how they work, the ecosystem within which they live, and in how they relate to other species within it.

Flowers have developed intelligent ways to get birds and insects to pollinate them as they themselves are mostly rooted to the same spot. They have developed such things as colour, smell and pollen to attract creatures that will help in the necessary cross pollination process. These relationships are symbiotic, in that there is benefit for both parties in the relationship.

The tolerances within this aspect of primary intelligence are incredibly fine in order to keep the system in balance. Humans, however, are able to upset that balance in the short term due to both their skills and high degree of mobility. They are able to introduce themselves and other species to different parts of the Earth but often with disastrous effects. Alternatively they often cross breed different species, again often with equally disastrous consequences.

This is not very intelligent behaviour.

The way nature deals with these things is by a slow process of merging and evolving, and not by brutal shock treatment.

Creative Intelligence

The next level of intelligence is termed 'creative intelligence'. This is where species begin to develop skills and arts that may, in some way, make them less subject to their ecology, or in some way enable them to control or regulate it. An example of this is the beaver that builds great dams in rivers in order that they may control and regulate the flow of water around their habitat.

Chimpanzees which have learnt how to use tools in a simple way by inserting twigs into an ant nest, knowing that ants will attack the invading twig, is another example. By attacking the twig the ants become attached to it and the Chimp then pulls the twig out of the nest and eats the ants.

Then there are the monkeys in Japan that have learned how to wash potatoes in salt water to get the mud off them before they eat them.

The species with the greatest amount of creative intelligence are human beings. Their creative abilities are far ahead of any life form on the Planet for humans can build, invent, and regulate their environment to a great degree to change their living circumstances. They can even build rockets to escape the planet's atmosphere.

In the deeper aspects of intelligence this may or may not be regarded as being intelligent, but for the purposes of this section it is definitely a use of creative intelligence. Nothing else on the Planet has this faculty or developed to anything like the same degree.

The use of this intelligence seems to be governed by the higher systems of brain, mind and mentality.

Humans can also choose how to use this creative intelligence, i.e. they can be creative in either a creative or a destructive way. Witness the fact that humans build and create monuments of great beauty and awe, such as the Pyramids of Ancient Egypt or the Taj Mahal, or compose music that can have within it certain healing properties. Or they can build weapons of war that can cause mass destruction in the blinking of an eye.

Creative intelligence is therefore a step up from primary intelligence, and it is clear to see that humans are the pathfinders of this form of intelligence.

The key issue with the development of this particular kind of intelligence is to do with responsibility. If the gift of Creation is to enable the gifted themselves to become creators in small, great care is needed to make responsible choices in the exercise of that creative faculty. It can be used for either life giving or destructive purposes.

True, creation processes work by giving and evolving life through the process of refinement. Humans would be wise to take note of this principle for much, if not most, of what they do in modern culture is anithetical to that motive. If humans are not careful they make real T S Eliot's vision of the Wasteland by their own hand. However, they can also create works of awe, wonder and beauty, if they choose. They can cause inspiration, delight and happiness, not only for themselves but for all they come into contact with – if that is their pleasure to do.

Spiritual Intelligence

This form of intelligence is the most rare and high, and because of its fineness it is the most difficult to see or prove. It has elements of the other two forms of intelligence in full measure but also has another element which forms the essence or core of its being.

This form of intelligence is unique on this planet to human beings, and yet is very rarely accessed for real by people. Those who do are the people who have creational awareness, sensitivity and knowing about the true divinity and order of life.

These are the masters, the sages, the knowers, the saviours, the wise ones, the pathfinders, the mystics, the healers, the bastions of truth, and true, living freedom.

The key features within spiritual intelligence are things like integration, connection, natural charisma, humanity, samarital nature, compassion, mental healing, visionary awareness, forgiveness, mercy, kindness, generosity, inspiration, allowance, encouragement, radiance, vibrancy, and much more.

All of these qualities are just that – qualities. They are not the produce of the ego or identity, nor are they selfish and self-serving in their application. This kind of intelligence always looks to the bigger picture and the greater good rather than one's own immediate and personal needs. Service is at the core of the activation of this kind of intelligence, together with the wanting to be useful to a higher cause. This is not to do with martyrdom or slavish addiction to a so-called point of principle or honour. It is simply the desire to serve the needs of higher things and the seeking of ways to be embassy for those things.

Spiritual intelligence is not remote or ethereal, in the common usage of those words, but is intensely practical. Its expression would vary from person to person, for all are unique in their make up and talents, but the core out from which it would come would be the same for all because it would be driven by the same motive.

Each person has within them, by design, the ability to activate and release this spiritual intelligence. It is the home of the evolutionary urge of the human design and species. There is, however, no guarantee that it will be released or activated because it entirely depends upon what the person does with themselves as to whether they become a living beacon of truth or not.

This type of intelligence pays no recognition to titles or material demand for there is no possibility of perversion of truth at these levels. In any event, there is no desire to claim or prove anything, for people at this level are awed and humbled by the magnificence of Creation and feel themselves to be a small thing within a very big thing, rather than the other way around.

Recently there was a film released called *A.I.* – Artificial Intelligence – where a very advanced robot boy tries to become a real live boy and feel the real feelings that such a boy can have. This research into AI has become a real obsession with many scientists trying to find out whether such intelligence can be created.

But, why?

Who, after all, would want artificial intelligence when there is such deep and profound intelligence available inside each and every person? There is a magic light inside everyone to offer and share with the world, if people open themselves up to what they have already been gifted.

Perhaps the sequel to the film *AI* should be called S.I. (Spiritual Intelligence)?

What a great gift to have. What hope it offers to the world. What a waste it would be not to use it.

The higher cause entrusted this higher part of itself into human beings to help them on the evolutionary journey that they are on. What a mistake it would be not to keep this gift in safe custodianship. What a crime it would be to keep it sequestered away and never use it for fear of losing it or making a mistake.

The key to unlocking this door is ...

Love.

Not the Hollywood kind.
But the holy kind of the love of causes.
Not causes in terms of issues as a first principle.
But *the* Cause.
That which caused all to exist and loves all that IT created and blessed.

To serve and be that cause is the highest intelligence aspiration there is.

And ...... it is a very bright thing to do!

Assimilation

*The mind is everything. What
you think you become.*

Buddha

*Appreciation is a wonderful thing, it makes what is
excellent in others belong to us as well.*

Voltaire

This subject provides clues and insights into how knowledge and development occur, according to inclination and level of accomplishment.

This chapter begins with an analogy about food.

When humans eat food they are, in effect, doing three processes. Firstly, they are breaking the food down into its constituent parts. Secondly, once this is done, they assimilate what they need from the breakdown of those parts. Thirdly, they eliminate those parts that the body has no need for by way of waste products.

The first thing to note about assimilation is that a person can only assimilate ingredients from food according to what is in it. Perhaps that is an obvious point, but it is nevertheless a very important one. This principle applies, in fact, to all experience and not just physical food, for there are many other kinds of food such as ideas, beliefs, philosophy, religion, and so on.

To continue with the analogy of food for a moment, a person cannot assimilate what they need from food if it is not present in what is being eaten. Conversely, they can and do assimilate what is in the food. Thus if a person eats nothing but junk food it is unlikely that they will assimilate enough trace elements, minerals and vitamins because such food has very little of these elements present within it. On the other hand, they will absorb much fat and carbohydrates as junk food has plenty of that within it.

Animals and plants know this principle extremely well indeed, for they know how to get what it is they need from their diet in order to be healthy. Humans, on the other hand, have become largely divorced from their natural sensitivity and detection systems, and therefore are generally no longer sure what they need. Mostly they go to the supermarket and buy what is on offer or what they fancy that day.

Much of the food today is filled with such things as additives, preservatives, artificial sweeteners, colours, chemicals, and so on. These then get assimilated into the body and often cause side effects, which in turn cause health problems. These can have genetic and other side effects, especially when they are combined with other influences such as drugs and prescriptions.

For example, there is a growing threat that more and more women will start to become infertile due to the fact that there are traces of the contraceptive pill in urine that is flushed into the water system. As much city water is recycled, in some cases up to seven times, there remains within the water small concentrations of the contraceptive pill. This in turn can affect other women who subsequently drink tap water, and because the water has traces of the pill within it they can effectively be 'put on the pill' simply by drinking 'tap' water.

The principle here is that a person assimilates what they come into contact with at all levels.

So: -

You are what you eat.
You are what you drink.
You become what you think about.
You are like what you like.
You become what you do.
You repeat what you know.
You become what you process.
When you mix with certain things they mix with you.
When you don't mix with things they can't mix with you.

It is sometimes said that someone who mixes with money a lot has the smell of money. This is no doubt true, as is the fact that human thinking and physical processes are definitely governed by what people eat and drink, just as what they think can govern what it is they choose to eat and drink and why. Also thinking and behavioural patterns, social exchanges, feelings and beliefs, passions and fears, aspirations and doubts, abilities and talents, insecurities and faith, are all influenced by who and what a person comes into contact with.

People therefore assimilate what they get close to. After all, there is no point going to live with the Inuit to learn Swahili, and there is no point in asking a Kalahari bushman to teach a person the piano. No amount of calculus can teach a person to appreciate great art, nor can all the laws in the world enforce freedom on its people.

Things go with things, and so it seems that humans are here to assimilate things from their experience and, indeed, be a crucible for things seen and unseen. What is meant by unseen are such things as qualities to do with the pedigree of being human. However, like the physical aspects of the body, people do have a choice as to what they introduce into themselves. What they choose to mix with will govern the results of that mixing.

Eating cyanide means death to the physical body. Perhaps hypocrisy and cruelty, for example, mean erasure to the higher parts of oneself? Alternatively, perhaps compassion and care may lead to continuance after the death of the physical body?

The journey of life here on Earth is to become similar to what it is that a person wants. The key in this is to be as natural as one can to who and what one truly is at every level. There is no point in trying to be like everyone else. They are probably having enough trouble being themselves without having others to compete with them as well!

This speaks therefore of being similar not familiar. For familiars are those ugly things that are carved on the outside of churches to give warning as to what happens to a person if they are familiar with their gifts, or if they assimilate unfortunate influences in their lives.

Osmosis wasn't, as far as I am aware, an Egyptian God, but osmosis is a godly process by which we absorb and assimilate foods of every kind. The ancients spoke of being eaten alive by the gods as being a state to aspire to. Therefore be careful what you eat, because you don't want to be eaten up by nasty gods like bitterness, regret, resentment, hate or guilt. Far better to be 'eaten' by humanity, love, hope, warmth and compassion. For I have a sneaking suspicion that Osmosis may indeed have been an Egyptian god and that he / she was the god of all these qualities.

Perhaps Osmosis was the god of how we absorb the future?

Interpretation

What is now proved was once only imagined.
William Blake

All meanings, we know, depend on
the key of interpretation.
George Eliot

There is the often held view in humans that they are the cause and the causer of their own experience. Whilst this may be true as a secondary principle, in that they have been gifted choice of action in a unique and special way, it is not true as a first principle. For the parameters and laws within which humans may exercise those choices are ultimately outside of their control. All they can control is the choices that they make, and from there the consequences of those choices naturally flow.

It is therefore important for humans to realise that what they actually do is interpret and translate signals and forces that they pick up on, both individually and collectively. Human beings are therefore like a radio set in that they pick up and play out the signals that they have tuned themselves to receive. They cannot respond to what doesn't exist, and as such they are subject to the greater influences and signals that the Universe sends their way.

The freedom for humans to respond is multiple but subject to the laws and perceptions that the human race's current situation allows it to have. The problem comes when humans make assumptions and wrong choices as a result of misunderstanding the dynamics at play and the polarities that they live within.

An example of this type of misunderstanding occurred at the end of the Second World War. The allies were closing in on Japan via the Pacific and it was really only a matter of time before Japan was defeated. The Japanese psyche is one of not surrendering due to loss of face, or Bushido, as it is called. However, the allies did not understand this psychology and therefore put an ultimatum to the Japanese for them to surrender or face the consequences.

Faced with this unacceptable ultimatum, which would mean loss of face, the Japanese had to try and find another way around it, and so they sent back a message in Japanese that could be interpreted in one of two ways. One was that they were refusing to surrender, and the other was that the Japanese were *unable* to surrender (meaning they needed another way to end the war, without such a direct surrender, in order to save face). The Allies, not understanding the concept of Bushido, therefore put the first interpretation on the message and assumed that the Japanese wished to fight on. Shortly thereafter the atomic bombs were dropped on Hiroshima and Nagasaki and the world was never the same again.

The point of this story is to illustrate the faculty of interpretation and how crucial it is in understanding the human condition. Humans are constantly receiving messages and signals at many different levels. The human body works totally by this interpretation and response system to help people live and survive. This works internally, through such things as the nervous system and the operations of the brain, to the digestive system, the immune system, and so on. It is a miraculous system of call and response, which works in direct response to signals received from outside, from fear to love to pain to joy and so on.

Often humans interpret the response required for those signals correctly, and often they do not. Everyone has stories where they have got it spectacularly right and spectacularly wrong. Or, more accurately, the consequences were useful or not useful.

The point here is that humans live in a response machine. They are not a causing machine as a first principle. Humans cause by their responses to things. This understanding is crucial, for otherwise humans misinterpret their own position in the bigger picture. Yet they clearly have a very powerful role to play on this planet, where response to those incoming signals is concerned, for the range of options available to them and the power involved is huge.

Therefore the requirement on people to exercise their choices responsibly is also huge. The weight of evidence suggests that since the upping of the potency of these upgrading and refining signals 12,000 years ago humans have not, in the majority, exercised those choices wisely. The primary reason for this is that humans have mainly been selfish with their choices and egotistical and immature in their behaviour.

They have been given an upgrade in their faculty to help with the interpretation of these new incoming signals but it seems that they have not yet properly learned how this faculty works, and perhaps not read the instructions that came hidden within the model they were given properly!

There is clearly nothing wrong with the human faculty per se – it is how it is used that matters. Perhaps, to a degree, it is inevitable that humans make mistakes in using this new supercharged possibility while they find out how it works, what it can cause and what it might be for.

It seems that many people are now realising that they need to mature and find their true place in the larger scheme of things. Humans are not the centre of the Universe but they are an important part of this part of it. They have a crucial role to play in the custodianship and stewardship of the next phase of evolution of life on this planet. In order to play their part they need to be able to interpret the signals coming their way better than they currently do. Not only that, they need to be able to send better signals out to the Universe about their intention and response.

This point is brilliantly illustrated in the opening sequence of the film *Contact* when the journey away from the Planet is one back through time (as the universe is receiving signals from the Planet). The most recent signals it receives from Earth are ones of deafening noise and a cacophony of dispersion. Gradually, as the camera travels further out into space, this noise lessens. In watching the film there is the sense of relief when the Universe no longer can receive signals from Earth. That ought not to be the case.

Yet things can change. The true and natural path exists and has been pointed to and shown by many throughout the course of history.

The faculty of Interpretation will guide people for, having been on an orbit away from themselves and their true place in universal affairs, humans are now at a turning point of history and evolution. Either they will sling themselves out into the oblivion of extinction or they will use their follies and errors as a kind of slingshot, galvanising force back to the journey of becoming who and what they really are NOW.

There is no doubt that the human race's interpretation skills – or lack of them – has led them into the deep crisis they now face.

However, crisis can lead to cruciality, and it is in times of cruciality that the real and deep and profound changes in alignment can be made.

The human race is in such a time right now and everyone can play a part in this change of polarity. Many are awakening to this rising call of consciousness.

The signal that all are trying to translate and interpret is one of recognition of what our true pedigree is, together with an urge to upgrade and refine.

Within that desire lies a brilliant unknown and unwritten future for all.

The way to help the future is to find out how to interpret what it wants and then try and be the same as it. This is something that people can be/do. Creation put the ability to interpret the future in each and every person, and that faculty is awakening in its hour of need.

The human race can rise to its possibility if they can phoenix out from their ghost-like past into the next phase of their journey.

The clues are all there in our physical and spiritual DNA. We simply need to find out how to interpret it.

Talent/Latent

It takes people a long time to learn the difference between talent and genius, especially ambitious young men and women.

Louisa May Alcott

Concealed talent brings no reputation.

Desiderius Erasmus

This chapter uses a curious inroad into exploring the esoteric nature of being human, and that is the anagram relationship between the words 'latent' and 'talent'.

Consider how apposite the anagram is when thinking about how close the words 'esoteric' and 'latent' are, for at one level both words mean 'hidden' or 'out of ordinary sight'. At the moment of conception each human has, coded within its unique life beginning, the genetic coding for all sorts of things about themselves. Their gender, hair colour, eye colour, height, shape, bone structure, fingernails, vital organs and everything else. It is quite extraordinary that all this information is contained in one cell when the sperm and egg meet and the genetic exchange and marriage takes place between them. What can be more esoteric than that?

In that micro world of hidden codings and signals, the map of who and what a person is and what they can become is etched out in quite a miraculous way. Alongside all the physical attributes are laid many other abilities as well; for example, the ability to communicate through language, emotions and feelings, certain unique individual characteristics, from traits and abilities to natural inclination, and so on.

All this exists in one cell that could easily sit on the top of a pin and that a person could never see with the naked eye. For who and what a human being is, and what they could become, is much more latent and hidden at this point, for it is the moment when they are least physical. What then happens is that, over the next period of time in the womb, the embryo receives nourishment, and via the process of cell division and ever-increasing differentiation and specialisation it grows into a baby. When they are ready to embark on their journey outside the womb they are then born.

Yet the basic building blocks of who and what they are already exists in that first moment.

It could be said that humans are almost pure latent energy at that time. Latent energy is a form of energy well known to science, and the hidden energy that exists within the relative stability of physical forms is absolutely massive. Einstein discovered this when he came up with his stunning equation of: -

$$E = MC^2$$

This says that the amount of energy in any physical body is its mass times the speed of light squared. A person doesn't have to be Einstein to realise, therefore, that the latent energy within a human being is absolutely huge. Yet that equation just represents the amount of physical energy. What about other kinds of energy that are locked up in people that they may not know about, be in touch with, or know how to activate?

What of emotional energy, intellectual energy, creative energy, spiritual energy, and no doubt many other kinds of energy, which are subtle and variant in their natures and expressions? What are the natures of these energies, and does the equation apply uniformly to all kinds of energy? Are the laws of physics constant throughout the Universe? For example, what if the equation worked differently for spiritual energy? What if, because of its fineness and potency, the ratio was: -

E = MC to the power of 26, as in there being 26 letters of the alphabet?

There is so much that humans don't know, and therefore the power of what they could be and become is much more unknown than known. Perhaps we need to free ourselves from what we think we know and be open to the fact that there are possibly many different levels and laws within creation. Like driving a car, it can only be filled with the performance level fuel that the model can handle. There is, for example, no point in putting rocket fuel in a Vespa motorcycle.

Reverting to Einstein for a moment, it is said that he was once confronted by a group of scientists who were determined to prove some of his theories wrong. His response was that he wished he were as certain about one thing as they seemed to be about everything! His researches had shown him that humans live in a vast, intelligent Universe and he was truly awed and humbled to the point of realising that the little he did know was infinitesimal to what there was to know.

Without that kind of reverence, what often gets supplanted in its place is arrogance. For despite his own wishes, Einstein's brain was removed when he died, and there were then disputes as to its ownership and whether it could be used for experimental purposes to find out how and why he became a genius! How can a person own another person's brain?

Yet the out of control of claims of rights of ownership applies at many levels, for currently there are attempts to put patents in place in respect of genes and their processes. Before long love will also be subject to copyright and patent protection! For if there is profit to be made then there's always someone willing to find a way to make it.

What becomes patent or obvious in people's lives, and what remains latent, depends upon what is promoted and what people relegate in themselves. By dint of human evolution it is clear that humans can choose to be agency for either fortunate or unfortunate aspects in the human condition. People can choose to be kind and compassionate or greedy and selfish. The amazing thing is that it doesn't need a University degree to do either. In fact that applies to the truly most important processes in everyone's lives, which is to do with what they activate in themselves. Qualities come out from the University of Life and not from having a diploma.

Qualities are the most enduring things of all. Yet, like all things, these Universal qualities need to grow or they themselves die or wither in this quadrant of the Universe.

This isn't saying that a person shouldn't go to university or that higher education is bad.

There are therefore, certain traps in pursuing the necessary exigencies in living. If a person develops certain systems from latency that are on a different plane or energy system to other ones, then there is a consequence to be realised in making such decisions. It is often said that a person cannot serve two masters, or they can't ride two horses in the same race.

This understanding is reflected in the story of the *Widow's Mite* from the Bible. In simple terms, the important Pharisee sits at the front of the church and tells God what a good person he is and how he gives a good amount to charity from the earnings he gets. Basically he is full of himself. Whereas the Widow sits at the back and only gives a mite, which is a tiny amount. She gives all she can but she is humbled and yet genuine throughout her life in what she does, as opposed to the Pharisee who is two-faced and hypocritical.

The story goes that God is much more pleased with the widow's gift, for it is not the amount that is given that is important but the place that it comes from. Surely it is more than coincidence that *mite* anagrams to *time*? Perhaps it was, in truth, that the widow gave more of her time to God than the Pharisee who was a 'Church only' religious person.

True talent is at play all the time in the person; it is either active or in latency waiting for something to trigger it into action. It is not a switch-on-switch-off thing, like going to Church on Sunday as some kind of insurance policy against whatever else it may be that the person has done throughout the rest of the week. Nor does doing something from guilt or obligation trigger something of a higher nature from the person either.

The thing that seems to work best is genuineness – which seems closely related to the word 'genius' by something more than mere chance. And by some stroke of genius that is exactly what the next chapter is about!

Genius

Conceit spoils the finest genius. There is not
much danger that real talent or goodness will be
overlooked long;
even if it is, the consciousness of possessing
and using it well should satisfy one,
and the great charm of all power is modesty.

Louisa May Alcott

Aptitude found in the understanding
and is often inherited.
Genius coming from reason and
imagination, rarely.

Marcus Aurelius

The common perception of geniuses is that mostly they are people who are born with a special talent and are therefore somehow different to the rest of the population. In truth that is not the case, for a genius doesn't have more natural abilities than anyone else. Rather they have simply activated more of the talents that they have been gifted. This small yet important distinction is crucial in locating a starter platform from which to proceed in researching this subject.

Otherwise there is an 'us and them' psychology created, because geniuses are regarded as being different to the rest of the population and are regarded as having been born special.

In one sense, however, they are born special, unique and individual, but that is because everyone is. The key lies in finding out what a person is naturally like and then developing those inherent abilities to their optimum level wherever possible.

For some people this will mean making breakthroughs and discoveries in all aspects of human endeavour. For others it may be something completely different. What is important is the process involved and not the results as a first issue.

This is where individuality and freedom of expression become sacrosanct, for without that there can only be a situation of conformity and generalism. Indeed, when looking at history and the lives of some of those who have activated their natural talents and genius, it is mostly through non-conformity and a willingness to pursue what they are driven by that they find out who and what they really are.

This is difficult to achieve, for the education and social system is organised in such a way that pupils are treated much like the assembly line method of making cars. Each year the same syllabus is taught by the same teacher who is trying to turn out the same model. The next year they move down the assembly line a bit further where another set of engineers (teachers) do another set of processes towards producing the final model.

This assembly line way of working, whilst being efficient in turning out numbers of end products quickly, nevertheless means that there is a lack of individuality. It also means that it dulls down creativity and individuality.

This system often forces the students to learn something that they don't have a natural aptitude or passion for. This can only dissipate the energy that the person has by channelling it into areas where the person has no natural flare or ability. What is needed are safe and pressure free ecologies for young children to explore and find out who and what they are and what they love to do and have a natural aptitude for.

Genius is like a garden in that there is a two-stage process. First of all it is necessary to find out what seeds have been planted in the garden. Having done that it is necessary to see what kind of ecology those seeds need in order to enable them to flower and flourish to the fullest.

It is appreciated that this is not necessarily an easy thing to do in a world run by economics. What is being asserted is not necessarily a revolution where the education system is concerned – at least not as a starter premise. Rather a review of the value systems and priorities at play so that the true importances can be placed at the core of that system rather than at the periphery as an afterthought.

If everyone thought the same thoughts and did the same things, it would not take long for all to be rather bored from the lack of variety. After all, it is well known that unless there is a great variety in the genetic pool of any species then it is not long before stagnation and extinction ultimately occurs. Why should human beings be regarded as being any different where this is concerned?

A person is a bit like a ruby gemstone when thinking about the processes of their life. Rubies are used in making lasers, and the way it works is that light is pumped into the ruby until it is saturated and then bursts out in laser form. Unless the rubies are standardised in size and shape, which they are for industrial usage, then the light that emerges from each ruby is unique in its expression and intensity.

This is a crucial concept to consider in researching individuality and genius. If this was applied at individual level then the type of light each person produces would be unique to them, according to their nature and experience.

Genius is quite close in structure to the word 'genes'. Could it be more than mere coincidence, therefore, that as each person is totally unique in genetic structure, they are also unique in the genius that each one of them has to offer the world?

Attitude

It is very important to generate a
good attitude, a good heart,
as much as possible. From this,
happiness in both the
short term and the long term for both yourself and
others will come.

Dalai Lama

Attitude is more important than
the past, than education,
than money, than circumstances,
than what people do or say.
It is more important than
appearance, giftedness, or skill.

W. C. Fields

This feature is perhaps the most important of all when considering how certain systems within the human become activated or not. As is sometimes said, attitude governs altitude – how high a person goes is determined by their address and actions in life and how they live that life.

Perhaps a curious place to start is from a numerological assay from the alphabet. There may be no more than curio factor in what is to follow, but then again there may be more.

Assume that each letter has a percentage value ranging from A = 1% up to Z = 26%. So the table would read as follows:

A	= 1	N	= 14
B	= 2	O	= 15
C	= 3	P	= 16
D	= 4	Q	= 17
E	= 5	R	= 18
F	= 6	S	= 19
G	= 7	T	= 20
H	= 8	U	= 21
I	= 9	V	= 22
J	= 10	W	= 23
K	= 11	X	= 24
L	= 12	Y	= 25
M	= 13	Z	= 26

It is possible to play with this grid and see what the numbers reveal about words

For example, *hard work* yields 97%.

Or *bullshit* equals 103%. Beware of people who promise more than they can deliver!

Amazingly *attitude* gives up the exact amount of 100%. Quite extraordinary!

If is taken to mean stance, address or approach then it can be seen that attitude really is a governor and overlord that conditions and shapes not only what people do, but also who and what they are and what they may become.

Attitude is an inner alignment that affects any outer action or portrayal and so is beyond opinion or any kind of dressage. In this regard it was said that the reason why the pectoral was worn around the neck and over the chest in Ancient Egypt was not simply decoration but rather a test of attitude. If someone was who and what they said they were, then the stones on the pectoral would light up when the person put it on.

They were truly meant to be an illumined person and therefore fit to lead. With highly conductive atmospheres it would have been possible to see the person's degree of illumination by directly observing their aura, hence the origin of the term 'illumination'. However, as with many esoteric human faculties, such as the finer senses of smell, hearing, clairvoyance and sight, it appears that these abilities have largely been abandoned or at least reduced down to a much more carnal or physical level.

This created the need to introduce more physical means of measurement and assessment, which in turn became even more reduced by the introduction of bloodline inheritance of authority.

The Japanese have a saying that the battle is won or lost with the first look in the eye. That speaks of an attitude for what looks out of the eye is the whole stance and will that a person holds. Everyone from boxers to businessmen knows this to be so, for an averted gaze speaks of lesser will and posture.

What then is attitude? Perhaps by way of analogy maybe attitude can be likened to the rudder on a ship, for it is the guide that governs the direction that the ship, or in this case the life, will go in. It sets the course and the way ahead, determining what routes are important and why.

On any such journey from A to Z there are always many, many adjustments or fine tunings that are needed along the way. The truth is that nothing in nature grows in straight lines; everything grows in spiral formations. Whilst the goal may be clear, the method of getting there always involves taking into account the unknown and the unexpected.

A person's attitude to life and what they do is very important indeed, for without having self determined what this is, it is almost like sailing on the high seas in a ship without a rudder. If this is the case then the ship is at the mercy of the elements and can in no way steer itself away from bad circumstances nor find the point it was trying to reach. Is this not also true for a life on its journey if it hasn't decided what is important, not only for the life itself but the context within which it lives and finds itself?

It is amazing when surveys are carried out about things like the meaning of life, life after death, God, and so on, that many people say "Don't know" to the questions asked. There are two kinds of 'don't know'. One is good in the sense of not jumping to conclusions, but the kind of 'don't know' here is the unfortunate kind for it speaks of not having thought about it, considered it or researched it. It is that kind of 'don't know' that damages the rudder of a person's purpose, whatever that may be. This inevitably leads to abdication of choice, on the one hand, and responsibility on the other.

This in turns means that the person then surrenders their purpose to others and ends up with the situation that although the person thinks and believes they are in control of their destiny and life, in truth they are not. If a person looks below the water line of their life they will see that their original rudder has been replaced by one put there by others. This is going to take that life to where those who put the substitute rudder in place want it to go and not where the life was destined to go on its own unique voyage of discovery.

It is a useful exercise for a person to pause and reflect for a moment about how many real decisions they have made in their life. In what context were they made? What were the choices available? How big was the list of options? How narrow was the opportunity? What was it premised against?

From this it might be seen that throughout the course of a life there may be several pivotal or key decisions made at various crossroad points. Most of these tend to be centred around which direction a person is choosing to take. How many are taken from the place that a person desires to come out from in doing what they do? This speaks of an attitude in process.

Here are some questions to enable a person to examine their attitude. What is important to discover is not so much the answers that are come to but the process had in getting there.

What is your attitude to your life?
What is your attitude to God?
What is your attitude to your gender?
What is your attitude to work?

What is your attitude to life?
What is your attitude to death?
What is your attitude to religion?
What is your attitude to the future?
What is your attitude to the Planet?
What is your attitude to politics?
What is your attitude to evolution?
What is your attitude to euthanasia?
What is your attitude to money?
What is your attitude to capital punishment?
What is your attitude to global warming?
What is your attitude to your spirit?
What is your attitude to other people?
What is your attitude to yourself?
What is your attitude to history?
What is your attitude to life after death?
What is your attitude to evil?
What is your attitude to your mind?
What is your attitude to healing?
What is your attitude to clairvoyance?
What is your attitude to love?

Most important of all, what is it that formed those attitudes? Further, did you know what your attitude was to these various matters before the questions were posed?

Finally, what is there about your attitude that you would wish to change, and how and where would you start to bring this into effect?

Inspiration

If you aren't in over your head,
how do you know how tall you are?

T. S. Eliot

Just don't give up trying to do
what you really want to do.
Where there is love and inspiration,
I don't think you can go wrong.

Ella Fitzgerald

Inspiration can almost be broken down to read Inspire At Ion, and so it is another of the ION words to do with being charged, lit up, enthusiastic and driven by a sense of purpose. Inspiration is truly a thing of the light, for when a person is truly inspired and lit up by something there is a presence or charisma about them.

This is often seen in children about very simple things and is much more common in the early years. It can, however, become dulled down as children become more 'adult' and familiar with the simple pleasures of life.

This experience is often felt when a person returns back to their earliest schools and places where they grew up and are astounded at just how small the play areas were compared to how they remembered them. How could something so small have seemed so large at the time?

The fact is that inspiration has a way of expanding the physical domains of things, making them appear far bigger than they actually are. That space is filled with the Oxygen of ideas and inspiration. The greater the magic the more there seems to be space for simple things to exist.

This precious fuel, however, often gets suppressed or crowded out inside the human race's lust to achieve, acquire, get ahead, make progress, and so on. Exigent living tends to squeeze the magic out and thereby makes things more physical and clunky rather than electric, fizzy and bright.

As the saying goes: 'All work and no play makes Jack a dull boy.'

With a lack of inspiration that is exactly what happens. The lustre of life becomes dulled down by the weight and oppression of too much to do or too much responsibility. Therefore it is vital to always keep a space in life for doing what one loves to do. That way a certain buoyancy and lightness is maintained that can help keep the person above the fog of general everyday existence level living.

It is therefore good to make a list of things that make a person feel inspired, and out from that list to then make time for those things to happen.

So, to get this process moving, here is a list of 21 things that make you feel inspired. The only thing is you need to write them!

1.
2.
3.
4.
5.
6.
7.
8.
9.
10.
11.
12.
13.
14.
15.
16.
17.
18.
19.
20.
21.

Try them individually, in groups or all together. Whatever works! Be inspired. It prevents global warming, helps make poverty history and stops comets from striking the Earth. Well, OK, that may be an exaggeration, but it does prevent gloom so maybe it can influence the weather?

If you don't want anyone else to rain on your parade then why should you rain on your own – or anyone else's for that matter?

So, how many trombones will you have at your parade?

Illumination

He whose face gives no light,
shall never become a star.

William Blake

Only in men's imagination does
every truth find an effective
and undeniable existence.
Imagination, not invention,
is the supreme master of art as of life.

Joseph Conrad

Illumination is regarded as being some kind of enlightened state or elevated human development, and it clearly is. But perhaps not in the way that people often think.

Illumination also means, in the literal sense, a bright light. A bright light can come from two sources, either inside or outside. Both sources of light change the ecology and awareness of the organism to which it relates.

Firstly, an external form of bright light has the effect of waking up the person from a state of sleep, especially if it is bright enough. For example, if someone is asleep and the curtains are drawn to show a really bright sunny day, then it is very rare for the sleeping person not to wake up, rub their eyes and move from a state of sleep to wakefulness.

This suggests that light is a more powerful state than darkness and that it causes the human systems to move from being in a state of torpor to one of activation. However, in order to do so a person has to be in a position to see this external form of light, otherwise their systems remain shut down.

Mostly people do not see the brilliance of life before them, and so they are literally walking around asleep with the curtains drawn over their eyes to such a degree that they only see the grey, the humdrum and the ordinary. They fail to see the miracle of their existence and so they exist in this half-light where nothing much impresses them because nothing much is seen as being special.

Things only change when there is some life changing moment that causes them to appreciate things in a different way. This often occurs when people face life-threatening events causing their values to change and for them to see the world differently. However, the world hasn't changed, it is they who have changed. Therefore the external source of light has switched something on, much in the way that lights outside a house enable the person inside to see what is outside at night.

The second form of illumination is that which exists on the inside of a person. In this analogy a person is regarded as having a fuse-box on the inside with lots of switches that can be turned on or off. As the various switches represent natural qualities of illumination, such as warmth, kindness, compassion and humanity, their natural position is on, and when on they cause the person to see the world in an illumined way.

However, most people tend to choose or allow these lights to be switched off and so tend to see the world through a glass darkly. Because they themselves are switched off they cannot see the beauty in other things and other people. Yet all they have to do is act as they truly are, which is full of light and warmth, and they will then see the world in a completely different way. The world will also see them in a different way.

This sounds easy and simple, and in a sense it is for it is natural. However, to act this way genuinely does take a large amount of development and skill. For to rise above selfishness into selflessness is a rare and truly illumined way of life.

Yet if a person stops and assesses their reality it makes perfect sense and the rewards are great. Like attracts like, and if a person gives out light and warmth then they will attract the same back to themselves, both from other people and from Creation itself.

This change in perception is neatly illustrated by the Earth's weather. When it is foggy or cloudy we say that the Sun isn't shining that day – but it is shining! It is simply that we cannot see it because of the fog or cloud that is in the way. The Sun, therefore, is a constant source of light and warmth to the Earth, even at night! Without the Sun there would be no life on the Earth whatsoever.

Yet there is life, and life on Earth is the Earth's fulsome response to the gift of light that the Sun gives. The Earth's illumination lies in the expression it gives to the light it receives from the Sun.

When human beings remove the layers of fog and cloud from their vision, they too become prisms rather than prisoners of the light. For like a true prism when white light is shone into it, it transforms itself into the truly amazing sevenfold expression we call the spectrum. In doing so the original light somehow appears to be magnified and made even more beautiful.

Humans can do this too, should they wish to be embassy and agency for the light. All they have to do is act the part and they will surely see.

Passion and Compassion

Out of chaos God made a world,
and out of high passions comes a people.

Lord Byron

Have compassion for all beings,
rich and poor alike;
each has their suffering.
Some suffer too much, others too little.

Buddha

This chapter refers to the two sides of the inner life; the brother and sister of what drives a person to be whoever and whatever they are and why they do what they do. Both are needed in equal and full measure for the person to be able to express their own individual uniqueness and brilliance. For passion without compassion is cruel and compassion without passion is inert.

Mostly in the modern world people are too busy to stop and think about the deeper issues of life and therefore tend to have passion about things that aren't that important. Some people, for example, are completely passionate about their football team or train spotting or collecting stamps or similar. This passion can even become obsessive in the person if they are not careful. The problem here is when it becomes delusional and/or psychopathic to such an extent that the person becomes a danger to themselves and other people.

Passion is a high-octane fuel that needs to be used carefully and wisely. After all, there is no point in putting rocket fuel into a car as the car will not be able to handle it and will blow up. Passion needs to be used for specific purposes that, like the rocket fuel, enables the person to escape the gravitational pull of ordinary life and enter another realm.

Passion is something that enables a person to respond in ways that are unexpected and non-conformist. If a person lacks passion they will be more concerned with what other people think of them rather than responding to the need that the situation before them requires.

It is a propulsion and a compulsion in that it charges and powers the blood, flooding the person with chemicals and the urge to do something to assist the thing that the person is passionate about.

A person can, however, be passionate about anything they want to be, and they often are. This suggests that people have a choice about what they become passionate about, and what that is depends upon what they have been programmed and primed towards.

Many people are passionate about religion, and usually this is a particular form of religion in that they are taught to believe certain truths about God and existence from their parents and religious leaders. This can often lead to a degree of fervour and ecstasy, or even extreme fundamentalism, because they have become programmed to believe in their faith to the exclusion of all others.

In such cases their passion becomes so pronounced that it squeezes out any compassion or tolerance for different belief systems and, indeed, will often seek to eradicate different views by such things as a crusade or holy war. Yet surely a holy war is in itself an oxymoron, for how can one seek to convert others to a truly religious life by the use of force? Or where animal rights activists seek to maim or kill people who carry out experiments on animals. They are clearly passionate about what they perceive to be the wrong done to animals in the so-called furtherance of human health and beauty, but does this justify the actions they take in 'revenge'?

As Gandhi said: "If everyone takes an eye for an eye then before long everyone ends up blind." For how many wrongs does it take until there is a right?

This suggests that the use of passion without compassion is like touch paper to tinder wood. In such circumstances it can easily become misdirected and arbitrary. No-one can say that people like Hitler, Stalin, Attila the Hun and Genghis Khan lacked passion and conviction about what they did. However, they became blinded by this passion into being convinced that they were right about what they were doing, which then gave them the mandate to effect their plans in whatever way was necessary for them to do so.

Passion should therefore not be confused with high levels of testosterone! Testosterone is a natural male growth and sex drive hormone that increases in potency as the male of the species moves from an immature to physically mature state. It creates a ripening into sexual maturity, but there are a number of side-affects that go with that process. For example, it causes males to be territorial and competitive as they seek to establish themselves amongst their species and find suitable mates.

This is in its most basic physical form, and human beings are no different from other species in this regard. Women are also most aware of the process going on in men as they themselves move into sexual maturity with the increased production of oestrogen in their own sexual maturing process.

An over production of testosterone or a failure to moderate its affects can be dangerous because it can lead to aggressive and confrontational behaviour, especially towards other men, but also often towards women. Such behaviour is clearly a misplaced use of what is a natural potency and vigour, especially when one considers that human beings have developed very dangerous tools and weapons with which to confront each over.

Many despots, who are invariably male, clearly have an over production of testosterone. This gives them a craving for power and a lust to prove themselves to be the biggest and most powerful male of the species. This competitive behaviour applies at many levels, from politics to sport to education to work to religion and more. It even applies to the human race's relationship with nature where humans try to 'beat' the forces of nature by developing systems of agriculture and energy use that subjugate the forces of nature to the will of human beings.

This is folly because, in the long run, the forces of nature are much more powerful than a male hormone that it is out of control. Ultimately nature will and does find a way to counter balance this aggressive influence.

Therefore it is quite amazing to think that many of the world's problems are caused by the over production and failure to regulate a male hormone. Unless men choose to be governed by a higher source of power, they can only be governed by a lower one. Testosterone was, and is, clearly essential to the establishment and continuance of human life, but clearly the time when it was the key player in governing human male behaviour has passed. Men need to moderate the influences that their hormones have on them, or else things can only get worse as the competition for resources and territory escalates.

Men need to take a different road from the one that assumes that lots of territory, plenty of power and wealth and lots of children, are the key signs of their potency, virility and success. They need to soften this thrusting and assertive nature into something that has a greater awareness and long-term view. Curiously enough, passion is something that can help in this.

Passion, unlike testosterone, runs cool rather than hot. It is moved by things rather than trying to move things. It is therefore free of ego and identity and acts in an impersonal rather than a personal way. As such it would help to moderate and channel the urges that men naturally feel, not only from their hormone factory but from many other things they feel as well.

Passion gives the context and framework within which men can act safely and feel good about doing something useful and constructive, rather than feeling they need to prove themselves to be better than others. A sure sign of this occurring is when men work well together as part of a team in serving a purpose that is greater than themselves, such as working for a greater cause rather than their own personal gain and advantage. Another sign of this process working well is when men take counsel from and listen to women. In the testosterone ruled parts of themselves men do not like to listen to women because men always think they are right and that they need to assert this view of themselves otherwise they will, in their view, be seen to be weaker and lesser.

In fact if a person is truly passionate about something they will naturally be open to the fact that they don't know it all and will need to consult and work with others. For, if they care about the issue at hand, seeing that it gets what it needs is more important than getting an ego buzz.

Compassion should not be confused with sympathy or feeling sorry for something. It is a much higher state than that. It relates to, and indeed can identify with, the person or thing that the person feels compassionate about. It has a resonance with the other life and can therefore feel the feelings of the other person or thing, yet it does not assume or pry or interfere.

It somehow seeks out the way to assuage the need of the other. Sometimes this means that no act is possible to alleviate the pain or difficulty that the other may be suffering, but this in no way means that the compassion is any lesser.

In that sense compassion is quite neutral, but never is it cold. It doesn't put anything upon the other person or thing, nor does it have any requirement from it. It simply seeks to be an agency whereby the other may somehow find a way to be in a better state than they currently find themselves to be. It is therefore colourless and unbiased, and as such is never maudlin.

Yet neither is it detached and aloof, for to be so would be antithetical to all that compassion truly is. Compassion is the vine of life and feelings are what anchor and transmit it. Compassion sees the other face of itself in another, whoever and whatever that other may be.

Compassion never seeks to punish or make anything else lesser. Wherever possible it seeks to elevate and expand the realms of cognisance and consciousness, for in such domains real freedom lies. It will seek, wherever possible, to lessen pain and suffering rather than add to it. Sometimes its actions may be misinterpreted by those who do not share the same experience or the same level of compassion.

An example of this sometimes occurs in war when a soldier eases the pain and suffering of a mortally wounded comrade by delivering a coup de grace to end the unnecessary suffering of a friend. Many regard this as an unacceptable action and an interference with the God given right to grant and take away life. However, this fails to understand that life is much more than a carnal existence, so to consciously ease the unacceptable and irreversible pain of another is both compassionate and a mercy.

The measure of passion and compassion in a person lies not in what they do but in the reason why they do what they do.

If there is a reason why the Universe exists then the amount of passion and compassion in it must be infinite.

Why should we, therefore, be any different?

Being a Healer

Make a habit of two things: to help;
or at least to do no harm.

Hippocrates

The art of healing comes from nature,
not from the physician.
Therefore the physician
must start from nature, with an
open mind.

Paracelsus

This chapter looks at something very specific and advanced, yet from a very particular premise seeks to provide new insight into the subject matter.

When considering healing it is easy to think that to become a healer requires years of training. For to become a doctor, a reflexologist, a physiotherapist, a herbalist, or similar, requires years of apprenticeship as there is much to learn and know, both about the theory and the practice of these disciplines.

It is easy to think that healing is something that a person has to learn about or something to be acquired from the starting point of lack of knowledge or ability. However, healing is an entirely natural process and, as such, is open and available for all to practice. Healing is something humans are all very good at, for they all do it all the time.

Consider how many times during the course of a life a person may have scratched or cut themselves. Then think about how the body healed itself by closing up the wound, creating scar tissue and then slowly returning the skin to normal over a period of time.

Consider also the kidneys. They filter out toxins in the system and pass them out of the body on a regular basis via the urine.

Then there is the sleeping process that people go through every day. This process heals the tiredness incurred from the vigours of the day. It also rebalances and realigns so that in the morning the person is refreshed and ready to engage in the day ahead. It is quite extraordinary that a person lies down, shuts their eyes, surrenders to sleep and then, as if by magic, they wake up a few hours later and have been re-energised. This is almost miraculous when one considers it.

Then consider eating and drinking, for these too are a form of healing as they give the body what it needs from external sources. The body obtains different nutriments from different foods by assimilating what it needs from what is ingested. It is important, therefore, that humans eat the right foods to obtain these necessary benefits.

Hopefully from these examples it can be seen that humans all live in a non-stop healing machine.

At this basic yet profound level healing is not something that humans have to learn. The truth is the exact opposite in that some of the bad habits and practices people learn and develop undermine the natural healing properties that are endemic within the human design. Eating wrongly, drinking wrongly, sleeping wrongly, walking wrongly, and even thinking wrongly all contribute to disconnecting people from the natural healing energies inherent in the design.

These notions represent a starter inroad into the research of being a healer from within.

The next example of this is smiling. Consider how many times in a person's life they must have smiled. Unless they are a bit of a miserable so and so it must be countless thousands or even millions! Each and every smile is a healing, not only for the smiler but also the receiver. What a great technology!

It is well known that smiling releases endorphins into the bloodstream, and these natural chemicals have healing properties within them. Smiling also uses a lot less muscles than frowning, so it is good body economics as well!

Then there is what smiling signals to the receiver, which is a sense of warmth, intimacy, trust, inclusion and mutuality, and more.

The other great thing about smiling is that it is contagious. Try not smiling when someone smiles a big genuine smile at you. It is curious that only human beings tell jokes to each other to cause laughter. Why have humans developed this ability? It cannot be arbitrary because all cultures do it. It has even been proven that people who smile and laugh a lot live longer. Here's an example to see if it causes any healing!

> *A man looks out of his window and sees that there are two men robbing his shed. So he calls the police on the phone and tells the officer on duty what's happening. The officer on duty says that they can't send anyone round at the moment. A couple of minutes later the man rings back and tells the officer not to bother sending the police around as he has shot and killed both of the robbers. Next thing the armed offenders squad is at the house with dozens of men, helicopters overhead, the works. They go into the shed and catch the robbers in the act, alive and unharmed. The officer goes up to the man and says, "I thought you said you had shot them?" and the man replies saying, "I thought you said you didn't have anyone you could send round!"*

Smiling is, of course, just one feature by which humans act and interact that can have healing properties within them. Touch is hugely important in how people relate and communicate, and how they do this is very important for humans can cure or inflict by their touch. There is nothing more intimate than a person touching another.

Yet it doesn't end there, for there are the aspects of the eyes and the voice. Consider the healing properties of a mother's soothing voice upon her crying child. Or the look of reassurance from one person to another that lets them know that everything is alright and that they are safe. Healing properties indeed, and yet there is no actual physical contact. Or is there? Physics tells us that there cannot be a passage of force without matter to accompany it. Light comes out of the eyes and sound waves come from the mouth, so these can and do contain physical properties, even though they may be tiny and immeasurable.

As every good homeopath knows, in the healing worlds less is more in terms of causing profound and long-term changes. All the drugs in the world cannot cause the same effect as a look of love from a mother to her child.

What can be seen from this is that there are many, many levels to healing, from physical to emotional to spiritual and everything in between.

Then there are what can be termed qualities and their healing properties. The list of these is endless and so is their power. Kindness, compassion, generosity, humanity, charity, forgiveness, love, devotion, loyalty, humility, sensitivity, warmth, and so many more qualities. These are all things that humans can and do process. They are healing to people when they process them for themselves, and to others when they are in receipt of them.

These are all things that humans are programmed to process naturally, and everyone has experienced what a healing it is to have received these qualities from another person.

Perhaps, therefore, if people were more conscious of what they generate they would be more careful and selective about what they allow themselves to process. Not only do they have a chance of helping another person, they also help to change the world. Human beings are like nuclear reactors in that what they process they generate into the atmosphere. This can either be ecologically regenerative or pollutant. It all comes down to one thing, which is a person choosing what they will be a generator of. There must therefore be dozens of opportunities for people, each and every day, to change the state of the world by what they think and what they generate.

The next feature is to do with human beings using external aids to assist in the healing process. This includes everything from herbs and minerals to foods to stones to colour therapies to massage and oils to acupuncture and countless other processes that assist the healing process.

Clearly many of these external aids work wonderfully well, especially if administered by a knowledgeable and sensitive practitioner.

One feature that definitely causes illness is too much selfishness or ego. This can be either through having a superiority or an inferiority complex. The fact is that both are complexes. Nature, however, works through simplicity, even though some of its structures are, in themselves, incredibly complex.

It could be seen that much illness is introduced into the system by complications beyond the simple rules of healthy living, which are eat well, drink well, live well, think well, and do well. As to the rest, the best preventative advice is – don't!

It should be noted that the word *ill* begins with I. Further, it can be seen that too much I of oneself causes a person to be unwell. This is an important issue to face in the healing realms, for often a person by their lifestyle, attitude or demeanour causes themselves to get unwell. Until they take responsibility for their condition, they are not going to be able to effectively begin the healing and re-education process. This applies equally to an alcoholic, a person who is grossly overweight, a person with a bad back due to poor posture, to cancer, and many other kinds of illness. In many such cases the person needs to look at the I of themselves before looking to external causes. It could well be an external cause, but mostly, in fact, it isn't.

If a person substitutes the *I* of themselves in *ill* with *we*, they get the word *well*. For the best way for a person to get well is to see the healing process as a team effort between all parts of themselves. Often, in the treatment of illness, too much emphasis is placed on curing the ill or diseased part rather than seeing that that part is simply showing the symptoms of a deeper malaise or misalignment.

If a person is not careful they can isolate and disconnect themselves from the ill part by abdicating responsibility for and connection to it. Often they 'hand over' responsibility to the doctor and surgeon, whose primary modus operandi is to attack the ill part with symptom based treatment or surgery.

But the cause remains.

Experiments have shown that the mind and attendant faculties can, and do, play an important part in the healing process. Visualisation techniques have been shown to work well, especially holistic ones where the ill part is regarded as being part of the whole (factor We) and reintroduced to the essence of wellness from the whole.

At this point an argument may be raised that there are certain things outside a person's control that may lead to them being ill, and of course this is true in many circumstances. This includes many things, from genetically inherited defects to environmentally caused illnesses to allergies to dietary problems and so on. On the other hand, this is another opportunity to consider the '*we* factor in all this. For the *we* aspect does not only apply to the *we* of the whole of a person but also to the *we* of the whole human race and all that *we* have done.

Inside this search into looking at the human race condition it can be seen that much of what exists in the world today is a legacy of what has gone before. In fact, it all is. It is worth considering that whilst these causes appear to be outside the control of the individual victim of certain afflictions, in the bigger picture perhaps the occurrence of these afflictions or diseases may originate from misalignment of the human race's collective purpose and nature.

It is only when *we* take responsibility for how things are that real change can come about at a fundamental level. How change is resisted is that things are treated as someone else's problem. Whilst attempts may be made to try and help that problem at superficial level by treating the symptom, until such time as it is seen as the whole human race's problem then no real change in attitude will take place.

All the aid in the world is not going to solve the world's famine problems. This is despite the fact that there is enough food and resources to feed the world easily. Where the problem lies is in terms of attitude, for the wealthy fear the consequences of what might happen if they share not only the food and resources, but also the power. A hungry person is a disempowered person and thereby easily controlled and suppressed.

The other curio to mention here is the secret ingredient that is far better than any pill in causing a person to get

well; that is the letter W. If the letter W is placed in front
of the word *ill* it changes to *will*. It is well known and
accepted that the most important aid to getting *well* is
will, for without it patients invariably do not get better.
Thus the will to live is the most crucial cornerstone in all
aspects of healing.

This kind of will leads to a literal effect called
willpower. If this is strong enough it can reverse the
polarity or direction of an illness and start the person on
the road back to recovery. How this works is by setting
up a different flow of energy within the person, creating a
unified field whereby all parts of the person are aiming for
the same thing rather than pulling the person in different
directions. The unifying force or motive needs to be
sufficiently strong to cause unity amongst the different
members of the person, otherwise the magnetic lock of
the current condition could still hold sway.

Thus *will* is better than *pill*. Sometimes it just needs
will and other times it may need will and pill. But
healing should always start with will and never with pill
alone. There is never a situation where will should not be
involved in the healing process. Otherwise the patient is
there for the doctor rather than the other way around.

In this regard consider how the modern method of
women giving birth, whilst lying horizontal on a bed
with their legs strapped up above them, evolved.

It derives from King Louis XIV of France asking his
physician to design a 'system' whereby he could better
watch the birth process as an observer. This method soon
became fashionable and is the standard procedure today
because it enables the doctors to see and control better
what is going on from their perspective rather than the

woman's. Yet the law of gravity, and many thousands of years of practice, have shown that it is far more natural and easier for the woman to give birth in a semi-squatting position. She is then working with the forces of nature and not against them.

However, the system is the system and anything that challenges that convention is to be attacked. This happened in recent years with Michel Odent who advocated water births for women because it eased the birth process for both the mother and the child. The evidence seemed to support his ideas, but he was ridiculed as being some kind of dangerous maverick who was endangering the lives of the women.

Yet, what of the assembly line processes adopted in some hospitals today with tubes and goodness knows what else stuck into the baby, often before the mother even has a chance to touch it?

This example is mentioned for that very point, which is to highlight some of the processes that govern and control the whole health and well being area. Ultimately what governs it all, like everything else, is money.

For why do drug companies develop new drugs to treat new illnesses? Is it primarily to cure illness or is it to make a profit for the shareholders? When a new drug is found they are not shy about charging large sums of money for it. In fact, mostly it is priced in such a way that many of the people who desperately need the drug cannot afford it, particularly in the third world. A recent example is in South Africa with Aids drugs which are often priced at levels around $25-30 per pill.

The main point of this chapter, therefore, is to highlight the fact that the human is a natural born healer of unparalleled excellence. Human beings are the most finely tuned instruments ever likely to be found. However, like any such instrument, the tune that comes out from it simply depends on how it is played. Even the most brilliant Stradivarius can produce the most abrasive, obnoxious noise if the wrong person gets hold of it!

Each and every person is a healer. It is their birthright and natural born talent to do so. They already have the starter kit they need, and that is *themselves*. The great thing is that they can start practising with it *now*.

All they have to do is care and try.

Immunity

*Every human being is the author
of his own health or disease.*

Buddha

*The secret of health for both mind and body is
not to mourn for the past, nor to
worry about the future,
but to live the present moment wisely and earnestly.*

Buddha

*It is no measure of health to be well adjusted to
a profoundly sick society.*

Jiddu Krishnamurti

Immunity is an evolved natural defence system that has developed over the course of human and planetary history as much as any other aspect of life. It operates at many levels, from biological to physiological to social to religious and even to esoteric levels.

As an example, early humans had immunity from the use of the wheel or controlling the use of fire. In art there was immunity from portraying perspective until new techniques were learnt during the Renaissance.

What then is immunity?

In simple terms it is a defence and blocker or prevention system that protects the host organism from invasion and tries to isolate and incapacitate any invading alien influence. For example, when people get an infection the immune system goes into operation to attack and expel the invading bacteria. It responds to the signal of an invader presence and then tries to attack and kill that invader influence by producing natural antibodies.

Humans have evolved their immune system response at many levels over millions of years out from their experience of living. This immune system development has generally evolved slowly, according to what it is that humans have come into contact with and their gradual adaptation to these influences.

However this is not always the case, and every so often pandemics occur when a completely new virus appears or a new strain mutates into a form that the human immune system can't 'read'. Sometimes these outbreaks are human caused, and these can show how the immune system adapts according to the environment within which it exists.

For example, the Native American Indians had no history of being in contact with European diseases. When the Spanish went to America their conquest of the people was made very easy by the fact that the natives immune systems could not cope with all the new diseases the Spanish brought with them, such as smallpox and venereal disease. Accordingly they were mostly wiped out because their mortality rate for some of these diseases was approaching 100%.

Curiously enough the process did not work in reverse, which must say something significant, i.e. the Spanish were not wiped out by Native American illnesses as there were very few of these.

Experience fashions immunity in many ways. Some examples for consideration of how it can and does evolve are as follows:

Immunity from Innocence
Immunity from Love
Immunity from God
Immunity from Knowing
Immunity from the Truth
Immunity from Continuance
Immunity from Hope
Immunity from Humanity
Immunity from Hate
Immunity from Cruelty
Immunity from Judgement
Immunity from Compassion
Immunity from History
Immunity from Greed
Immunity from Selfishness
Immunity from Feeling
Immunity from Death

Here then are some salient points to consider:

The first is that for a very long time humans were unaware that they were different in essence to the flora and fauna life with which they shared the Planet. They were obviously different in appearance but they were not outsiders looking in. They were an integrated part of the whole system. They were also immune from the idea of control or dominance over the Planet and the flora and fauna life. In short, they practised sustainability without knowing what it was.

The second point relates to of some of the appalling things that have blighted the human journey due to low and base behaviour; such things as war, pollution, the plundering of the Earth's resources, and so on. It must be that these events could only have happened because humans had become immune to both the higher orders of nature and its principles as well as the higher systems of themselves.

Otherwise how is it possible to explain torture being in the world? How else could it be possible for one person to inflict pain deliberately on another simply for pleasure? Or how can the killing of animals, solely for personal gratification, be regarded as being a sport? This does not say that the act itself is right or wrong, but it does suggest that the reason why these things are done gives them some kind of placement outside the natural order and moral code of life.

Nothing in nature kills another thing for sport.

Nor does it torture.

There are things that do go on in nature that may seem to our value judgements to be cruel or unfair, but they all happen for a reason inside nature's permissions and laws.

It was when humans ate from the tree of knowledge that they became *aware*.

When someone becomes aware of something they are no longer immune to it. This is the whole principle of how Voodoo magic works, for a person has to be aware of what is intended to happen to them before the spell can have any effect.

In this developing awareness humans learnt that there was choice, and if there was the opportunity of choice then they could exercise some control over their circumstances and their surroundings. They could be the cultivators of their own possibility and thereby not subject to the same laws as everything else on the Planet in the same way.

Humans began to actually build immunity to the Planet itself. How else could the ever-increasing rate of disconnection to the host on which human beings live be explained? Humans are polluting, destroying ecosystems, causing mass species extinctions, consuming the natural resources of the Earth, drastically reducing biodiversity, over populating, releasing dangerous chemicals into the environment, interfering with the natural patterns and cycles of the Planet, and so much more.

Humans have largely become immune to the fact that the Planet and everything on it is a live, sentient organism that feels pain when humans do what they do.

Nevertheless humans plough on in their obsession for growth and progress. Humans have become like a cancerous growth on the Earth and, as such, they surely cannot expect the Planet's immune system not to activate and begin to treat humans as being alien invaders, can they?

Cancer is an unnatural process inside the body running out of control and threatening the life form within which it grows. Perhaps this is the actual truth of what humans have become to the Planet. A system that worked well originally has somehow developed a negative mutation and now threatens the life force processes of the host on which it lives.

Whilst it is true that humans could suppress certain laws that govern them for a short time, once they discovered that they had awareness and choice these laws and Nature's parameters and controls could ultimately not be avoided. Plus, the longer the misalignment and abuse the greater the price there is to pay.

Human beings would do well to take stock of where they are and where they are heading. The false dawn of their naïve perception that modern science could give them a bug free, disease free, table of plenty future is clearly born of ignorance and arrogance.

It is not merely coincidence that the number one disease threatening the human species in the last twenty-five years is called AIDS – Acquired Immunity Deficiency Syndrome. Within this time bomb of a disease is the fact that the human immune system is under attack. AIDS is not the only immune system invader that threatens to undermine the health and well being of the human race as a species into the future.

Modern children's immune systems are becoming more and more weakened from the experience of being born into a world whereby the immune system is undermined by the use of chemicals and toxins. This means that children suffer more and more from things such as asthma, tuberculosis, leukaemia, cancer, bronchitis, influenza, and many more ailments than ever before.

What has recently been discovered is that part of the problem is not just the squalor inside some inner city environments; ironically it is also caused by over sanitised circumstances. The use of bleaches and chemicals in the home, air conditioning, and all the rest of it, might kill the bugs (until they develop resistance to it, that is) but they also undermine the human immune response. Not only that but because humans don't interact with the earth and dirt they do not get the benefit of some natural immune bolstering that comes from mixing in small amounts with that which might attack them later.

This was the whole point of the medical breakthrough in the use of vaccinations. It was discovered that to have a little bit of something made a person immune to larger attacks of it later in life. The body has a memory and genetic map of how to deal with that particular invader having already dealt with it once before. Nowadays, with more and more of the world's population living in cities, the stresses and pressures on the immune system are enormous. In some ways children are much more vulnerable today than ever before. This situation is bound to worsen because the perceived panacea to all ills —antibiotics – are now being found to not be the magic answer many thought them to be as, in many cases, the bugs have become immune to their use.

With this cocktail of out of control influences on the march it is quite possible that some genetic mutation of diseases could rebound on the human race in a major way. Consider what might happen if a deadly virus like Ebola was crossed with an airborne virus like tuberculosis. That would be an absolute disaster when considering how it could be transported around the Planet in aeroplanes before anyone could do anything about it.

Human beings live on the thinnest piece of rice paper imaginable.

We need to bolster the immune systems of ourselves and the Planet before it is too late. One way to do that is to return to a more natural way of living. In seeking to conquer the Planet and the forces of Nature humans are, in fact, undermining their own place in the scheme of things. The Planet does not allow species to live on her unless they serve some kind of function and purpose. If this is so then humans have no mandate to come along and wipe out other species simply because they feel they have the right to do so.

Finally, it is important to note that it is possible to become immune to negative or positive influences in equal measure. What a person has become immune to depends upon how they have arranged themselves.

It is possible to be immune to:

> Not caring
> Not trying
> Not loving
> Not sharing
> Not helping
> Not accepting
> Not believing
> Not hoping
> Not being warm

It's easy to do. For many people do it. But it is easier in fact and more energy efficient to do the opposite. How?

Just try doing any or all of them by removing the word 'not' from in front of them!

How to Be your Own Saviour

Worship is transcendent wonder.
Thomas Carlyle

Nobody can give you wiser advice than yourself.
Marcus Tullius Cicero

This chapter could confront certain views that some of the world's religions and the people in them may hold. However, the purpose of this chapter is not to seek to destroy the platforms upon which these structures have been built but rather to check their foundations, just in case they might not be quite as sound as previously thought.

One of the key ways that many of the world's religions bind their members in to the fold is to place much emphasis on the saviour principle. This is basically to say that the religion itself is built around the concept that a specific person who lived some time ago was divine and therefore a saviour of and for the human race. Therefore if a person today wishes to be saved then they should follow the example and path shown by this 'saviour' and they themselves will also be saved.

The difficulty in this approach, however, lies in interpreting the path and way demonstrated by the so-called saviour. For most of these saviours didn't write anything down or record their teachings; this was done by others who lived in later times.

To further help solve this problem, the religions of the world have such people as priests, rabbis, mullahs, and the like, to tell people what they should think, do and say and when and where they should do it and how and with who, if they wish to follow the true way of this saviour.

The main problem with this is that it usually creates a classic divide and rule scenario whereby the innocence and / or ignorance of the masses is played upon by the leaders for their own control purposes.

This in turn inevitably creates a culture of leaders and followers with always fewer leaders at the top and more and more followers the further down the pyramid of power one travels. It is little wonder, therefore, that the followers of these processes are called a 'flock' for they are indeed treated like sheep! The reasoning here being that sheep do not think for themselves; they let someone else do it for them and then follow where they are led.

The psychology hidden within all this is that a person can't ultimately save themselves. Only this dead/living saviour can do it by mercy and forgiveness of the poor soul who is following them. This then creates a whole culture of dependency and supplication for it causes the adherents to feel dirty and unworthy and in need of forgiveness and redemption in order that they may be saved.

Therefore the need to do good acts and good deeds is driven by the desire to be forgiven for their lowly status rather than wanting to do good deeds because it is normal and natural to do so. In truth there is no slate to wipe clean.

All that exists is what a person crystallises in themselves by reason of what they do and why they do it – no more and no less. The idea of sin is clearly a religious invention to keep the masses subdued.

Far better to consider that there are only two key factors that actually govern any life – choices and consequences.

Choices lead to consequences and consequences lead to more choices.

Don't let anybody or anything else try and save you. Only you can save you because, after all, only you know how you got yourself into your current mess in the first place!

Seven Pillars of Belief

We all have our own life to pursue,
our own kind of dream
to be weaving, and we all have the power to make
wishes come true, as long as we keep believing.

Louisa May Alcott

Belief consists in accepting the
affirmations of the soul;
unbelief, in denying them.

George Eliot

The title of this chapter is based on T. E. Lawrence's book, *The Seven Pillars of Wisdom*, and is an attempt to twin belief and wisdom together, for they are closely related.

Belief has to be an important cornerstone in a person's life, for everyone has a belief system of one kind or another, as how they live depends upon what they believe in.

Perhaps it is more than mere co-incidence that *belief* itself anagrams to *be life*. It does seem that what a person believes in or gives credence to they give life to. This opens up huge areas of research into things such as the power of the mind, the placebo effect in medicine, psychology, religion, and much more.

With regard to the Placebo Effect, what has been found is that, even if a person is given an inert pill, if they believe it will work then, more often than not, an improvement in their condition will occur. The same effect has been shown with Voodoo in that once a person becomes aware of a curse being put upon them they become vulnerable to it. It has also been argued that many of the so called remedies claimed in homeopathic medicine may in fact be due to the placebo effect in that if a person believes that they are taking something to make them better then it may do so even though the "remedy" is not causing the cure, but the belief in it is.

What follows are seven possible pillars of belief itself:

Pillar One   *Trust*

Trust is a crucial and fundamental cornerstone upon which the first pillar of belief stands. Imagine not being able to trust whether one was going to wake up in the morning, or that a person couldn't trust their heart to keep beating without them controlling it? A person can trust the fact that the Sun is going to come up again tomorrow, and they can trust that they are going to wake up in the same body! Imagine what it would be like for a person not knowing whether they were going to wake up as themselves or someone else tomorrow!

Trust is therefore inherent within the natural design and order of things in a very profound way. It also exists in more subtle realms, for it extends into all experiences, personal relationships, and so much more. The more people are able to trust others, the more they are able not only to believe in them but also what they are joined to.

There is a very clean and fresh sense with trust because there are no half measures with it. A person either trusts something or they don't. If they don't, they must be based in suspicion. Humans are not suspicious of certain permanent truths, such as the law of gravity or the four seasons, but they can develop suspicions about motives and the reasons for things.

It seems that the more people base themselves in what is natural, the more they can trust in those things and thereby the greater the chance to build their belief in the reasons for things and why they are the way they are.

Pillar Two   *Classification*

A great feature in building belief lies within the regularity and natural order of things. In short, things go with things. A baby very much begins its life by experiencing things that are either pleasant or unpleasant. It experiments through its senses to find out what it likes and what it doesn't like. Things are put in the mouth and sucked and eaten if nice or spat out if nasty.

This kind of simple classification process develops throughout people's lives in many different gradations. They sort things into groups according to what they believe about them. For example, they classify those people as friends who they believe in because of their experience of them. Others they classify as enemies because they do not believe in them or they do not believe the same things that they believe.

Thus all sorts of systems build up in a person arising from their experiences. But experience is always subjective. For example, people are often brought up in particular religious faiths and therefore that faith is what they believe in. They then classify not only themselves out from that experience but also tend to classify other groups as well. The same applies in terms of a person's job for a person, when asked what they do, will often say that they are a doctor, a housewife, a scientist, a gardener, or whatever. This is what they believe, for this is how they classify themselves.

Classification, of itself, is neither a good or bad process, but it does seem to be pivotal within the belief building process.

Pillar Three   *Experience*

This pillar is to do with the aspect of building a catalogue of attempts or processes that give a foundation upon which trust can be built, or seem to be well merited. The more something is known to be the case over a period of longevity, then the more it can be believed in.

For example, as a child grows it develops more and more belief in its physical systems and their ability to do – to run, jump, sing, make music, dance, write, and so on.

The wider the experience a person has the greater the net of belief that can be cast. This suggests that it is important not to be narrow in one's experience, for that tends to lead to such things as dogma and bigotry and they are not sound platforms upon which to base belief. It is said that travel broadens the mind, and there are many kinds of travel that can be undertaken to facilitate this process occurring, not all such travel having to be physical.

This is where people like Leonardo da Vinci stand out in world history as they were experienced in many fields of science and art. Out from that experience they were able to develop a belief system that was way ahead of their time.

It is curious that the word experience can be seen to break down as follows to give further insight:

Ex   -   meaning out from
Peri -   to mean the surrounds of many things
Ence -   to mean the essence being obtained

Out from the many surrounding activities, observations and discoveries into the way things work, a person can begin to appreciate the essence nature of what causes things to be the way that they are and thereby can they safely develop and grow their beliefs.

Pillar Four   *Understanding*

Understanding is a great antidote to ignorance, for ignorance is a great builder of faulty belief systems. In ignorance of the fact that the Sun is at the centre of the Solar System all sorts of theories were created as to how the Solar System worked and articles of faith and dogma were born out of those beliefs.

The same principle applied to Archaeology, for in the absence of any understanding as to how to date fossils until relatively recent times it was thought that the literal interpretation of the Bible was correct and that the Earth was thought to be only 6000 years old. Because the processes involved in the creation or establishment of the Universe are now better understood it is easier to show how it evolved over time.

It is the same with learning a new language. The more a person learns about its vocabulary, formation, structure and meaning the better able they are to understand it and thereby express themselves within it. In the absence of being able to understand the hieroglyphs on the Rosetta Stone it was only possible to guess what it might mean. Once the code was deciphered the meaning could be understood and the belief about what was on the stone could then be confirmed or rejected.

A small understanding can go a long way to both build valid belief systems and dismantle invalid ones. Sometimes this can happen more or less overnight. When Darwin first proposed his theory of natural selection, where evolution is concerned, conventional thinking was turned on its head and changed people's beliefs as to how humans evolved.

The same principle applies to dealing with others. The absence of understanding leads to judgement and this can only undermine belief. Yet with understanding comes better knowing about another and greater surety in believing what another person will and won't do.

Pillar Five   *Research*

This pillar is to do with hunting out the truth in whatever way one can.

This system looks at the way things work and why and is the discovery and learning process that incorporates everything from play to analysis and all things in between.

Research is the process whereby a person tries to get to the core truths and is the non-stop questing and questioning process to gather greater perception, evidence and understanding.

If things are not researched then the belief can only be shallow, and if the belief is shallow then the response out from that belief can also only be shallow.

Research is a great anti-shallowness process that always drives the person onwards towards greater revelation and connection and thereby fortifies, evolves and emancipates the belief system of the person from ignorance and prejudice to insight and awareness.

Pillar Six   *Detection*

This feature speaks of the ability of one's systems to be able to assess what is the deeper truth of what might be at play or what causes things to be a certain way. The key word within this aspect is 'training'. The more finely honed one's detection systems are the better they will work in helping to build the tower of belief in the person.

Perhaps Sherlock Holmes is a good example of training one's detection systems as he was able to form threads of belief that were more subtle and finer than other detectives. This was because he had trained his faculty to observe every nuance that others would miss.

If a person uses their systems in a general way then one can only form a general system of belief. But if they are used in a more specific way then a more exact, detailed and reasoned belief system can be formed. Further, the more well trained the detection systems are the better they are at also separating fantasy from fact. A loose and badly trained system can detect things that aren't even there! The detection systems feed back into the belief system and either creates a filter system that separates invention from fact or cause a person to believe in the tooth fairy or that one is the next messiah, or whatever!

Pillar Seven   *Surrender*

In thinking about the final pillar of belief there is a sense of things needing to come the other way, i.e. there is a sense that a person can't work all things out from the bottom up but that there must be a transcendent aspect to belief.

In this there is an acquiescent dimension to belief, or a yawing in the face of the bigger picture.

This feature is partly captured in the Bible story concerning Jesus and Thomas, the latter who stated that he would not believe that Jesus had risen from the dead until he saw him and put his fingers inside the wounds that Jesus had suffered. When they meet and Thomas confirms for himself that Jesus is alive, Jesus says to him that he has seen and believed yet blessed are those who have not seen yet still believe.

There is something within this that speaks of a platform that the life has built that allows for this kind of belief to be activated. It is not to do with naïveté or blindness, but rather an openness and receptivity.

There is an analogy within the process of surrender in war when the losing side, having fought the best it can, waves the white flag of surrender and thereby puts its trust in the winning side's compassion to treat it fairly.

If a person surrenders to something higher then it can transfer its purpose to them, providing they are prepared to surrender to its requirements.

Now that really is something to believe in!

This chapter is analogous to taking a glimpse through seven separate keyholes into a massive chamber of belief. Maybe it's like the story of seven blind men having gone off into the jungle, each having felt a bit of a new animal they have discovered. They then have to describe it to the king. Some say it is like a snake, others say it is like a tree trunk. None of those bits alone constitute what the animal is, but together they give a composite of what the whole actually is – an elephant.

What a person does is governed by what they believe in. If those beliefs are connected to more permanent truths, and more integrated with the cycles of how things work at a deeper level, then the results of both the beliefs a person has and the actions which they take as a consequence will be much more rewarding.

These seven pillars of belief can create in a person a temple within which great things can live. However, if these seven pillars don't do it, the reader is invited to find seven that do.

The future needs people who believe in it.

Without belief we can only ever be lesser than who and what we really are.

Inhibit the Habit and Don't Inhabit the Inhibition

How is it that little children
are so intelligent and men so stupid?
It must be education that does it.

Alexandre Dumas

It is easier to prevent bad habits
than to break them.

Benjamin Franklin

Each and every person develops habits, roles, patterns, and ways of going on that are adaptations born out of a survival instinct due to living in a largely unnatural and often hostile environment. Mostly people are not themselves and, if this is difficult to believe, a useful exercise is for a person to try observing themselves for a day to see how many roles and identities they slip in and out of during the situations and dealings they have. This includes when they are on their own! The vast majority of these roles are, in fact, mostly far too subtle for the person to see, otherwise how else could they have got a grip on them in the first place? Secondly, if they could see them easily then they could do something about changing them.

Most human response is governed by habit rather than natural inclination. This blocks the natural pathways of meaningful engagements, for people develop things like moods, demands, expectations and conditions, and all sorts of other behaviours that keep them from being themselves.

The keyway out of this state of affairs of perpetual imprisonment is through the exercise of choice.

Most of the time people do not actually choose to be how they behave, it just simply happens to them. This is why people say things like "I don't know what came over me." This is quite literally true for they have, by default, allowed a habitual response system to come into play rather than a self-elected one. The more this habit is reinforced the harder it is to break, no matter how much the person might want to. This is the key to understanding addictive and obsessive behaviour patterns, for the more something is engraved the more dominant and governing it becomes.

The first step towards remedying this is to realise that it is the case and to become conscious of it.

Once this is done then the dominant, active processes at play can be paused. This in turn creates an opportunity for selecting an alternative behavioural response. There is nothing wrong with being a sheep in one's behaviour, providing a person has actually decided to behave in that way!

Without this exercise of choice there is, in fact, an abandonment of responsibility and the adoption of pre-programmed automatic responses that simply reinforce the state of disconnection of the person from themselves.

Awareness is a very powerful tool for a person in helping to face the various situations that their life comes into contact with. Before finding oneself stuck in a non-chosen behaviour pattern it is therefore useful for a person to ask themselves some questions:

What is the situation I am facing?
How did this situation arise – what are the dominant causes?
What are the choices that are available to me?
What is the need I choose to serve?
How does that require me to be?
Which choice most closely fits that requirement?
How do I begin to put my chosen response into action?

This process may look somewhat sterile and inert on paper, but it does work if practised. It may appear clumsy and even calculated at first, but after a period of time it becomes much more live and dynamic. The more it is practised the more natural it becomes.

In this way habitual patterns of behaviour can be overlaid, changed and overridden in favour of more spontaneous and natural responses.

This then leads to the second aspect in this chapter, which is to do with not inhabiting the inhibition.

There is a very strong link between habit and inhibition, as the stronger and more narrow the habit life the greater the inhibitions the person will suffer. The reason is that anything outside of habitual response puts a person outside their comfort zone, and because of this they do not feel safe. In such circumstances they unsurprisingly become inhibited in their responses.

The way around this feature is to practise different kinds of versatility. This helps in giving the person a wider range of skills to select from in making a chosen response to any situation they face.

There are many ways in which to make small marks in this direction, for ultimately it is not really anyone else's censure and censorship that stops a person, but rather their own.

Here are some technologies to try:

Try speaking at different speeds and tones in different circumstances.

Try walking in a different way and style. See what causes what and use as appropriate.

Try walking a different route to work.

Brush your teeth with the other hand.

Dress in a different order to what you usually do, e.g. put the other sock on first or put your top on before your trousers or skirt, if you usually do it the other way around.

Answer the phone in different ways.

Smile at a stranger (with safety, of course).

Let your eyes be free to look up when you walk places.

Practise singing to yourself, even if you think you can't.

Imagine yourself in situations before you are in them, and rehearse the possible scenarios that may be at play and the choices you may need to make.

Make a list of what kind of things make you feel inhibited, and then draw up an action plan of how to shrink those things.

Find out what things give you natural confidence and try to find ways to do more of those things more of the time.

Learn a new word every day and try to find ways to get it into the conversations that you have.

Write your projections for the day at the start, and then at the end of the day write down your successes.

Look for examples in nature of the opposite to inhibition, and find ways to incorporate that frequency into your life.

The list of things to try is endless so find some of your own that work for you.

A person needs to grow these things quietly and effectively, for if they have developed habits and inhibitions over time then the chances are they have been there for years. Therefore it is important not to rush it and suddenly become an exhibitionist and loud-mouthed bore! That is not what is being said.

Quiet progress makes a loud noise.

Lastly it is important to say that habit, of itself, is neither good nor bad. What habit does is print the person in either a fortunate or unfortunate way. A person needs to choose habits that reinforce their purpose rather than weaken it.

It is therefore a good habit for a person to keep reminding themselves of their purpose and the reasons why they do what they do. This will help to weaken the influence of negative habits and assist in developing a better set. It will also help inhibit the inhibitions and thus prevent a person from making an exhibition of themselves!

Innocence and Guilt

The innocent and the beautiful
have no enemy but time.

William Butler Yeats

Every man is guilty of all the good he did not do.

Voltaire

What a fascinating combination this pair is! It appears that they have been a part of the human story for as long as humans have existed as a species; certainly in their latest modern form since the shift from hunting and gathering to agriculturalism.

These natures are all pervading throughout all aspects of human life, from birth to death, in deep and profound ways. They apply to everything from religion to the criminal justice system, to codes of behaviour and morality, and so much more. The criminal system, for example, works on the basis that there is a presumption of innocence until such time as guilt is proven beyond reasonable doubt.

However, since mankind's 'fall' there has somehow been an inherent sense of guilt within the human psyche that manifests itself in the concepts of things like sin, confession, punishment, penance, self-flagellation, and so on. All these behaviours come out of some kind of perception that the human is born dirty and needs forgiveness in order to find salvation.

The appearance of this concept of guilt must, to some degree, be linked to a diminishment of innocence. It is almost like a person can have 100% of any combination of these two states, from 100% innocence and 0% guilt to 0% innocence and 100% guilt, with every possible combination in between. It appears that the more 'modern' cultures have advanced the more they tend to veer towards the concept of guilt being the more dominant influence.

It is noteworthy that whenever new primitive tribes are discovered – in say the jungles of Brazil or Borneo – one of the first things their discoverers say is that they have an innocence and simplicity about them. By 'primitive' it is meant that they have not had real and substantive contact with modern cultures. Perhaps this innocence is quite understandable, in most cases, simply because they have nothing to feel guilty about. They have adapted to living in harmony with their surroundings and generally have no malnutrition, don't pollute the environment, there is no crime, and they don't suffer from over population problems or resource shortages due to exploitation. Yet Western cultures call *them* primitive!

Nature doesn't have guilt, and therefore it can only be a human learned response. A pride of lions do not feel guilty about killing a gazelle, nor do trees feel guilty about trying to get to the light of the Sun from the canopy floor. Magpies do not seem to suffer guilt for stealing shiny objects, and winter doesn't feel guilt for closing in.

The reason for this absence of guilt is that natural things operate within set parameters and controls. There are checks and balances to enable species that humans often regard as being competing to successfully co-exist. It is only human beings who have developed both the capacity and will to live outside of these parameters and seek to control the environment and the things that live within it.

This again refers to the origin of modern humans as told within the story of Adam and Eve. A key facet of this story relates to the forbidden fruit that Adam and Eve were told not to eat from the Tree of Knowledge. Despite this warning, they did so. The Tree of Knowledge, or Gnosis, gave them an insight into how the natural laws worked and how, if they chose, they could manipulate those rules for selfish advantage. This they choose to do, and this selfish behaviour was continued by their son Cain – or *I can*. It is worth remembering that Cain also murdered Able.

Once Adam and Eve ate the forbidden fruit they felt guilty and naked and wanted to hide, not in reality from God's wrath, but from the truth of their now disconnected state. No other animal has any inhibitions about being seen naked because that is how they live all the time! Yet there are so many confusing attitudes in the modern world about the human form and sexuality, which are all symptomatic of a much deeper malaise.

It is said that nature abhors a vacuum, and so in the absence of natural innocence it seems that humans have managed to supplant innocence with full blown guilt in its many and varied forms.

All of these forms take as their fundamental starting premise that there is something constitutionally wrong with human beings; that they are flawed, unworthy, dirty and in need of forgiveness by the all-perfect God who frowns deeply upon their imperfections. Meanwhile humans do not fundamentally change their behaviour patterns, and thus the guilt increases.

Humans have to deal with this contradiction by way of more confession or more gifts to charity and more foreign aid whilst they continue to exploit the parties to which gifts are given even more. This goes on in an ever-increasing downward spiral away from reality and truth.

There has to be something quite wrong when statistics reveal that the USA spends more each year on slimming aids than it does on famine aid for the rest of the world. Over 75% of the world's population hasn't got enough to eat, whereas the world's richest spend fortunes on trying to get slimmer due to over indulgence.

In truth there is nothing fundamentally wrong with human beings, despite such things as the Catholic notion of Original Sin. Look at a new-born baby in its innocence and purity and consider just how marvellous the design of a human being is. Reflect on all the fantastic capabilities and skills it possesses. The talents and abilities and ranges of versatility are simply breathtaking, and so the first natural response to life and existence would naturally be one of awe, wonder and pride and not one of guilt and shame.

The legacy of what humans have inherited through misuse of that design is something to seek to remedy, but that is not something to blame the design for nor, for that matter, the designer. The analogy of how this process works is similar to that of using a computer to download images from the Internet. It is possible to download any of the vast range of images available, from Encyclopaedia Britannica to paedophile pornography and everything in between. If it is the latter that is done, then it is not the computer that is put on trial but the user.

It is not the model or human design that is to blame for the state or condition human beings find themselves to be in but the choices they have exercised within the model. If the choices we have made have led us to a point of peril then, by logic, it says that the choices we make from here and into the future can lead us back from the brink as well. Not only that, but also to a world of harmony and integration where the natural friendship that humans can offer to the Planet and its people – to mean all flora and fauna life – would itself flower and bloom in a much richer way.

Innocence and guilt are human value judgements upon the merit or lack of merit of human actions. Either of these states can be avoided if a person simply seeks to be responsible and kind wherever possible.

Is there anywhere where that isn't possible?

The Truth

If the doors of perception were cleansed everything
would appear to man as it is, infinite.

William Blake

There are only two mistakes one can make along
the road to truth; not going all the way,
and not starting.

Buddha

When it comes to deep and profound matters concerning the business of living, the journey for a person ultimately becomes one of a search for truth. This journey is a process towards something rather than an end in itself. For truth is a relative property and any truth that is discovered depends entirely upon the approach used. To illustrate the point, try the following exercise: Get two people to stand opposite each other then get one person to place their arm out in front of themselves, pointing the arm at the other person, and get them to move their arm in a circular fashion. Then ask both people which direction the arm is going in – clockwise or anti-clockwise – and see what both people say. They disagree. Why? Because the position from which they both view the event is different.

Here is another example: Get three bowls of water from hot to medium to cold. Get one of them to place their hands in the hot bowl and the other in the cold bowl. Then get them both to place their hands in the medium bowl and ask them whether that bowl is hot or cold. Again they will disagree.

These simple exercises explain so much about the truth, opinions, world history, dogma, war, and so much more. The truth is that both people are projecting *their* reality on to *its* reality and therefore both are at distance from *the* reality.

It often seems that truth is something that people shy away from or dilute or alter in some way to suit their own reality. Not following the truth and its consequences has killed many people, but the truth itself never did. One doesn't see in the obituary columns that someone died of the truth. For the truth is that the truth is not a life threatening disease, although the way some people react it sometimes is!

Not only is truth relative but it is also a gradient. As in climbing a mountain, the higher a person climbs the more they can see of the surrounding area and the context of their climb. Until the person gets to the top they do not know exactly what the view is going to be like when they get there.

It is not certain whether the first or last step on a journey is more difficult. What is clear, however, is that without all the steps in the middle the first and last will never meet its joined destiny.

Conception

*Great indeed is the sublimity of the
Creative, to which all beings
owe their beginning and which
permeates all heaven.*

Lao Tzu

*The best of artists has no
conception that the marble
alone does not contain within itself.*

Michelangelo

This is where everything begins.

The word 'conception' is quite clearly made up of two parts: *concept* and *ion*.

It is therefore curious that one of the first attempts to find a simple set of laws that governed all things was called the IONian Enchantment. This occurred about 600 BC in Greece and became famous for its derived perception that if everything came from the same source then that source must ultimately be water.

Obviously we know today that this is not true, but nevertheless the deductive process of reasoning involved is, in fact, very advanced because the Greeks had no substantive knowledge of atomic and molecular structure or particle physics. Replace water with energy and perhaps the Greeks were not that far off the mark. Ultimately everything in the Universe is made up of various states and forms of energy, and it does appear that there are a simple number of laws that govern how those forms of energy exist and relate to each other.

As science becomes more sophisticated and advanced in its technological aspects, it is increasingly seen that the way the Universe works is simple yet incredibly intricate to the point of being intelligent under any measurement system of intelligence that might be used. As Einstein said, "God doesn't play dice with the Universe."

Perhaps the early attempts at what has now become a Unified Field Theory were well named in being termed the Ionian Enchantment, for everything begins (and ends up) in the Ionic realms.

What Conception says, at first level, is that before there was any ion to anything there must first have been a concept. If so, then where did that concept come from and how did it first manifest before even any *ion* part to it existed?

The term 'conception' is primarily used when thinking about the moment of fertilisation when the sperm meets the egg and they unify as one in exchanging genetic information to set the blueprint for a new life. However, it can apply to anything from ideas to Big Bang theories of how the Universe began, to composing music, and more. Everything has to have its origins somewhere and if things are traced back far enough they all begin in the ether or the unseen.

Whilst at the moment of conception there is clearly an exchange of physical data between the sperm and the egg, there is also something else that happens that is quite mystical, for ultimately it is the question of what is life itself and where does a person actually come from?

It is accepted that the physical act of sex (putting on one side for the moment test tube fertilisations) is necessary for conception to take place. Yet that is simply the physical cloak and opportunity for something profoundly esoteric to take place, which is the appearance of a new life.

No scientist can really explain what life is any more than they can explain what electricity is or what love is or what time is, let alone explain the purpose of why we are here and the mysteries of life.

Life truly is a mystery and is enigmatic and elusive to any bottom line definitions. The evidence of this can be seen when thinking about the fact of a person dying or 'passing away'. Where do they pass away to, and what is it that passes away? Whatever it is, it must be infinitesimally small for the body doesn't weigh any different before the moment of death or after and yet the person has gone, or at least their vital force has. It must come from somewhere and go somewhere.

Perhaps this is where it is possible to begin researching the prospect of life as being some kind of coding, in that all life is coded in certain ways to process particular energies and frequencies and thereby release certain vitamins from its experience.

Here are some questions to ponder at this point:

What were you before you were conceived?

Not only that, but *where* were you?
What was the Universe before Big Bang?
Where was it before Big Bang, and where did it get the stuff to go Bang with?
What and where was Creation before it was created?

These are both simple and complicated questions that merit some contemplation!

If all the ingredients of the Universe were actually present at the Big Bang it says that, in some shape or form, each person was there too, and so it must be true that each person is actually made of star dust! Everything has simply evolved and changed its form over time, and indeed continues to do so in a dynamic yet orderly way. On any close inspection it will be seen that at the core of Chaos Theory there is nothing but Order as far as the eye can see and beyond!

What can be seen from the ways that Creation and the Universe work is that there are fundamental laws by which they operate and govern their processes. The evidence suggests that there is intelligence within the system of how things are governed and how they work and that this intelligence is an evolving and a relative one.

Conception marks the beginning and birth of things, yet it is not possible to get something from nothing. It is better, therefore, to see conception in terms of octave or polarity change. In reality life and death are not opposites but are rather adjacent octaves whereby energy changes its form.

As one life ends another is about to begin and the whole cycle of birth and death continues from one domain to another, from one epoch to another, and one dimension to another. The evidence for this is becoming more and more accepted as scientists now begin to research seriously the concept (there's that word again!) of parallel universes to the one that humans occupy now.

They claim that quantum theory and the mathematics add up to indicate that it is possible. But then again, so what? Were you born out of quantum theory and mathematics or was it something else?

Conception isn't a quantum or mathematical equation.

It's the birth and affirmation of life.

So with this in mind, if you pardon the pun, go forth and multiply!

Can You Do it?

*People need hard times and oppression to develop
psychic muscles.*

Emily Dickinson

*The study and knowledge of the
universe would somehow
be lame and defective were no
practical results to follow.*

Marcus Tullius Cicero

The issues that the human race faces about the future,
both as a species and as individuals, are massive beyond
belief. At first glance it can appear that there is nothing
that can be done that will make any significant impact
whatsoever.

There is nothing that suggests that one person on
their own can do anything either.

Yet there is something they can be.

There is something they can become.

There is something they can believe and radiate.

There is something they can have belief about.

Each person can begin this journey in small by growing the care they have for life and the future.

Modern living is hard and harsh and deals from stress to stress. A person, therefore, needs to become a stress free zone and a safe haven for things of account.

They can carry the baton of light and hope so that those yet to come can see it appearing as they themselves journey to this planet to assist in whatever way they can.

The planet on which humans live needs more people to switch their lights on so that something out there can see that the experiment is coming right of its own account.

Bright things endure and offer continuance, and all the darkness in the world cannot blot out the light of a single candle.

It is not about being different to everyone else.

It is about being the same as oneself.

That will make the only difference that matters.

From that place everything wins, for it is the one and only thing that is clean.

You Attract What You Act

Birds of a feather flock together.
Great minds think alike.
Fools seldom differ.

People often say that they want to change. They may not be happy with certain aspects of their life and therefore wish to make improvements, refinements towards being happier in the general life circumstance.

Great!

However, what people mostly do not realise is that the reason why their life is the way it is comes from the fact that they have already become a magnet for what has happened in their life. In other words, their existing behaviour has caused their current situation to be what it actually is. Or, to put it another way, they already have what they want otherwise they wouldn't have it!

Now many would argue that this sort of statement is unfair or untrue because many people are born into unfortunate circumstances and can do nothing to change them due to the overwhelming external pressures that prevent them from changing them.

Wrong!

The reason they are, in fact, not able to change their external circumstance is the fact that they are not able to mount sufficient internal pressure to overcome the lock or hold that their external circumstance has upon them.

This is not saying that it is easy to change a person's circumstance, for the external forces at play are very strong and it often requires a superhuman effort to overcome these existing holding patterns. It also depends on what it is that the person wishes to change, for the power of the desire to change will be met in equal measure by the forces that do not wish the person to change either themselves or their circumstance.

What people need to realise is that their existing behavioural patterns cause most of the problems or things that they wish to change in the first place. Now it is admitted that everyone is a victim of education, custom and practice, social and religious expectations, peer group pressure, and many other fixing patterns of behaviour. These create great pressure on a person to behave in line with certain expectations of the society that they live in.

In short, a person is expected to conform and if they do not conform then there are certain consequences that they can expect, from social and religious exclusion to being ostracised, to punishment and even, in extreme cases, to persecution and death. With such a negative set of consequences awaiting those who dare not to conform, it is hardly any wonder that most people simply accept their lot and settle for what is dished up to them, drifting through life thinking that they can't make the changes they would like to make in their life or in the world.

Little do people realise that their behaviour mostly reinforces the very things that they would, with half a chance, change. As such they are faced with a stop situation that they think they cannot change. There are many degrees of subtlety to this scenario, most of which escape the person's awareness and perception.

Further, when a person seeks to make any changes to this lock situation, mostly the changes they seek to make are of a transient and superficial nature concerning the person's temporal and material situation. This relates to things like money, status, possessions, jobs and the like, and in seeking to make these changes a person is simply exchanging one set of conformities for another.

If these changes relate to creating a better life platform than the one the person currently has, then fine, for a stable and secure life platform is crucial if a person is to make deeper changes in their life. But if the platform becomes an end in itself then a person will simply alter their behaviour to meet the new requirements or needs in their life but they won't, in fact, change.

The point here is that we are magnets that work by the process of attraction and repulsion and that we are, all the time, sending out signals as to what we want and what we don't want. Things, therefore, respond to these signals with like always going to like. The problem here is, however, that people are mostly unconscious and unaware of this process and, therefore, it is mostly hit and miss and arbitrary for most people. Or at least they think it is. But nothing is arbitrary and therefore a person does get what they want because they are sending out subliminal signals as to what they want and these signals are being responded to.

However, because this process is mostly unconscious, people are not aware as to why the things that happen to them do so and they therefore mistranslate and misinterpret those signals. As such, rather than seeing these things as signs and opportunities, they tend to see them as events that are arbitrary and out of their control. This is an abdication of responsibility and causes a person to feel everything from inadequate to life is hard and not fair.

This is a big mistake.

Archimedes once said that if he had a big enough lever then he could move the world. In effect each situation that a person faces in their life is a point of leverage opportunity. The trick is changing the mindset to see that this is the case and, when this happens, then life becomes a series of opportunities rather than a series of problems. When this is done the energy of these situations changes polarity accordingly.

What does this mean?

Well it means that the person changes from being subject to situations in the first instance to being causative of the situations that they find themselves in. These situations then change from being solid and fixed to being fluid and mobile.

This is a massive change in perception and also possibility.

For when a person makes this switch they start to see that they truly do attract what they act.

The reason most people view their situation negatively is that they don't see this to be the case. Because of this belief the external pressures create a default reality, i.e. one that is imposed rather than one that is chosen.

This doesn't mean that some people aren't born into difficult or testing situations; they clearly are. In fact it is suggested that every situation that a person is born into is a testing situation, for extreme wealth is just as testing for a person as extreme poverty. The test is completely different in its manifestation but the struggle to find out who and what one is and is meant to be still exists in equal measure.

Further, the fact of not being born into a perfect situation doesn't seem to have prevented the great men and ladies of history from rising above the fog of prevention into being something of account, both for themselves and the world they lived in. They often used their situation as a point of leverage into something superior that transcended it.

How they did that was to try and see their situation for what it really was and then try to change it, not only for themselves but, more importantly, for the good of the world and for humanity.

Sometimes the best way to change a problem or difficulty is not by making it smaller but, in fact, to make it bigger because this creates a much bigger context within which to consider the issue. By making it bigger the energy field available to address the situation becomes bigger as well.

Examples of this are easy to find, and here is one from my own experience:

When I was exercising to keep fit I used to swim in a pool and do a maximum of 24 lengths with 3 lengths of front crawl followed by 1 length of breast-stroke. This was the only way I could complete the 24 lengths by doing this combination in 6 repeats. Or so I thought.

I then decided to do a Triathlon and this was going to require me to swim the equivalent of 60 lengths. This was before cycling 40 kilometres and then running a further 10 kilometres! This faced me with an obvious dilemma as I couldn't even swim more than 24 lengths front crawl without being exhausted.

This meant that I could no longer accept that my current abilities were to be governing. So I didn't, and because the needs of my circumstances had suddenly expanded massively I could no longer afford to think that my abilities were as limited as I thought they were. And surprisingly, because I had to multi-task my training to cover all three disciplines, my ability and stamina in all three improved beyond their previous best levels to a massive degree.

Therefore when I came to participate in the Triathlon I was ready. My training was good, my mindset was clear and I had even hired a whizzo bike for the middle section. However, what I hadn't counted on was getting a puncture in the first 2 kilometres of the bike ride and, because I didn't have a puncture kit with me, I had to ride the rest of the 40 kilometres with the back tyre 75% deflated. So by the time I finished the bike ride section the tyre might have been 75% deflated but I felt 100% deflated!

Somehow I managed to finish the run and when I crossed the line my arms and legs were covered in crystallised sweat. No doubt the fact that it was 80° heat had contributed to this but the effort needed had taken me beyond what I had prepared for.

The unknown is like that.

It doesn't demand that you enter it, but make sure you prepare for going in there properly and take what you think you might need.

And, if the going gets tough, remember the first thing you need to attract is that which lies hidden within you.

Being Settled

The important thing is not to stop questioning.
Curiosity has its own reason for existing.

Albert Einstein

Happiness is when what you think, what you say,
and what you do are in harmony.

Gandhi

One of the biggest mistakes that people often make when seeking to make changes in their life is that they start from the premise of what is wrong or what needs changing.

This is a bad move!

Whilst the premise of changing what doesn't work is a workable thesis it is, nevertheless, far less potent than trying to make a good situation better. And in order for a person to make a good situation better a person has to be settled with who and what they already are. This is paradoxical because why would a person perceive that they need to make any changes in their life if they are settled with who and what they currently are?

Well, life is full of paradoxes and this chapter seeks to address that very fact by asserting that you don't have to be bad to get better.

Now some may argue that their personal situation is so bad or bleak that they cannot see how they can regard it as being in any way fortunate or advantageous. It may seem that way but, in fact, it isn't because all realities are relative and if a person doesn't start from the premise that their situation is indeed fortunate then they are living in the wrong reality.

Here is some argument to substantiate the assertion being made here:

Firstly, a person can obviously read this book and is therefore blessed by the fact of having eyesight. Things would be a lot worse in their life if they were blind, and it is here that the well known saying, 'You don't know what you have got until it has gone' starts to bite. For people often do not value what they have until they lose it, and the reason for this is that they take what they have for granted.

In fact most of the time they do not even realise what they have because they never really sit down and consider the matter. Mostly they tend to consider what is missing or wrong, and this means that they can't see the wood for the trees. Not only do they not see what they already have, they also fail to see that they have all the tools they need to make the necessary changes that they want to make.

The irony that exists here is that people who have lost a faculty, such as sight, are often better adjusted and more settled than people who have all faculties working. Why is this? One reason is that if a person is coded to see and receive negative impressions then, if they have more faculties working, this logically says that they will therefore see and receive more negative influences in any given situation.

However, a person who has lost the use of certain faculties tends to be grateful for and value more the remaining faculties that they do have. As a result of this they tend to see and receive the upside of situations rather than the negative side. Lesser importances do not tend to obsess them as much as they do people who appear on the surface to have more going for them. These people, because their centre of gravity is based in dissatisfaction, tend to complain more about lesser things that are wrong rather than being grateful for the small things that are right.

In continuing this theme about being settled it is relatively easy to show that each and every person has something about which they can be grateful.

For example, a person may have a wife, husband, girlfriend, boyfriend or partner to companion them. If they do then they are very lucky, for presumably they entered the relationship voluntarily because there was a mutuality and companionship that they wished to share together. This is a very fortunate state of affairs and one that a person ought to be very grateful for.

Now some may say that they are not in any such relationship and claim they are entitled to say that they are clearly lacking or missing something in their life compared to the fortunate who are in such a relationship. Perhaps this is true, but then things could always be worse because at least a person can say that they are not in a relationship that is toxic or violent. Indeed they might have met someone who may even have murdered them or stolen all their property, so it is easy to be thankful for not having met the wrong person!

Other people may see that they are very fortunate because they have had children and they are proud of them and that their genetic line will continue into the foreseeable future. Those without children may see this as something missing in their life, but again things could be worse because some people have children who are ungrateful, bring shame to the family or even bully or are violent to their parents.

What is being said here is that no situation, of itself, is good or bad. As was said by Shakespeare, "Nothing is good or bad Horatio, but thinking makes it so."

Of course, it is natural for a person to want to change things in their life that give them stress or are unsatisfactory. What is being said here, however, is that the real power in respect of change lies in the psychology of making a good situation better rather than make a bad situation less bad.

The proof of this axiom lies in the following little test:

Write for 10 minutes about how things could be worse in your life. Do not in any way censor yourself in this process, and so you can write everything from saying that a sniper could have assassinated you this morning to your hand could have been caught in a car door and you lost a finger, to you may have been struck by lightning on the way to work and rendered blind as a result, or even killed.

Then spend 10 minutes writing down all the things that are good about your life. Again, do not censor yourself in any way and write everything that comes into your mind, from the fact that your heart beats over 100,000 times a day to keep you alive to the fact that you have enough to eat to the fact that you have never been subjected to torture in your life (if this is true).

Then after you have done this compare the two lists and write down separately what this exercise has shown you about your situation and how it may have caused you to see things differently from how you may have previously seen it.

Then, as a third part of the exercise, spend 10 minutes writing down the things you would like to see change in your life. Again, don't censor what you write and don't feel any pressure to write either lots of different things or deep and profound things. Just simply write what naturally comes up in you about it.

Hopefully the exercise will reveal that the desire for change will come from a different centre of gravity in you than simply starting from the platform of wanting to change things that may be perceived as being wrong or unsatisfactory.

There is a lot to be settled about in this world, for so far today the Earth hasn't stopped spinning on its axis, nor has the sky collapsed in upon you. The Sun has continued to provide light and warmth to the Earth and, as a direct result of this, there is still food and water available to you.

There are a great many blessings that each and every one of us can choose to count, if we so wish. But first we have to see exactly what they are and why we should be grateful for them. Otherwise a person will only ever see that their glass is half empty as opposed to the truth of the situation, which is that their glass is not only half full but is, in fact, overflowing.

Finally it is worth considering that all situations in a person's life can be improved or made better. If this is the case then what are the three key things that a person would wish to improve, and what are the three key things that are needed for each of those situations to be improved in turn?

Also, as a balance to this exercise about improving one's own situation, what are three things that a person could do to improve the situation for other people?

These things do not have to be Earth shattering; they simply need to be practical and do-able.

For improving the lot of others helps to improve one's own situation and also helps reinforce the view that, indeed, one is far more fortunate than perhaps one previously thought.

Now that's a settling thought!

Watch Out for Entropy –
It Could Kill You!

We live in a rainbow of chaos.
Paul Cezanne

Only entropy comes easy.
Anton Chekhov

OK, so the highlights of the book are as follows:

The world is in a mess.
The future is in a mess.
You are in a mess.
Entropy reduces everything down to chaos and disorder in the end.

Rather depressing then, isn't it?

Not a bit of it!

For out of chaos come more and better order, better form and greater freedom.

So don't just sit there; go and find some chaos and sort it out, will you?

And just so you know, you don't have to look or go that far to make a start!

Epilogue

Finding you in a world gone mad

It is hard to find oneself in a world that is clearly mad against what is natural where the human design and possibility is concerned.

The world is a very chaotic and dispersed place and therefore it is important to find some core stabilities inside the search and quest to be oneself and to be effective in what it is that a person chooses to do with their life.

Perhaps a clue lies in the fact that *finding you* anagrams to *unify in God*.

Now some may say that they do not believe in God and that there is no point or significance in the anagram. But everybody believes in something – even nihilists!

The point being that it is important to decide what to believe in, and to then try and get all one's systems pointing in the same direction in pursuit of it.

There are few people who do not wish to see a future that is better and safer than today.

It is not known if there is any specific culture that has or had a God of the future.

Therefore maybe it is time to think about what kind of God that might be.

It could, for example, be the God of the unknown.

If we are to have a future that we can all celebrate and be thankful for, then we need to find the ways and means to unify, both individually and collectively.

And if we do find these ways to unify, inside the belief and faith that we can all have for a better future, then maybe, just maybe the age of miracles and saviours might not be over.

And you, yes *you*, might be an example of both.

About the Author

Tony Kearney was born in New Zealand where he grew up and studied at University. Having qualified as a lawyer he then embarked on travels around the world before settling in London where he practised as a lawyer for nearly 25 years.

In his spare time he has been involved in many diverse activities and events in relation to matters of planetary and global change and has travelled widely taking workshops, seminars and giving lectures on topics from current world issues to personal development.

In 2006 he moved to Ireland where he furthers his work in the above areas as well as acting as a facilitator, trainer, consultant and mediator.

Boo! is his second book, his first being ***Who Owns the Future?***

See: http://www.authorhouse.co.uk/BookStore/ItemDetail.aspx?bookid=53656

Lightning Source UK Ltd.
Milton Keynes UK
29 October 2010

162087UK00001B/1/P